FURIOUS
A HORRIFIC TRUE TALE OF DOMESTIC ABUSE

T.L. Mackae

© 2025 Tallulah Louise MacRae

All rights reserved

First edition

Independently published

Paperback ISBN: 9798282600308

Hardback ISBN: 9798282855913

No AI has been used in the creation of this novel in any function or facility. I do not give permission for AI to be used on anything contained within these pages.

No part of this book can be reproduced in any form or by any means, without permission from the author. All photographs, artwork and words are my own.

Also, by T. L. MacRae

Non-fiction:

Conversations I'll Never Have

Conversations I Have in My Head

Furious: A Horrific True Tale of Domestic Abuse

Fiction:

Beware The Rosemond Ripper

Taking Melody

Author's Warning

Long ago, I believed that I was the one people would think of when they said things like, "If he hit her, I bet she said or did something to deserve it." I'm embarrassed by how long it took me to realise that no matter what I said or did, I did not deserve to be beaten or raped by my partner.

You, as the offended party, have the option to leave that person & relationship. You do not have to stay in a partnership of any kind you are not happy in. Allan (Not his real name. Names have been changed to protect the privacy of those who are legally entitled to it) was not being forced to stay with me, it was the other way around. However, if he was unhappy with me and of course to strangle me and rape me (sometimes multiple times a day), I couldn't believe he was anything but unhappy.

He could leave me for someone else, someone more to his liking. Happy in a new relationship. He kept telling me that the only reason he hit me was because I said things he didn't want to hear and did things he didn't like. Me. It was all my fault; everything he did and how he reacted. I was the problem, according to him.

Now, you might think I was wild and running around cheating on him with anyone who breathed in my direction or was kicking puppies. The simple truth is, I told him I wanted a divorce because I wasn't happy being in a relationship with him.

Funnily enough; being raped and beaten daily at points, made me not want to be in a relationship with him... How fucking selfish of me! How talking about my feelings and telling him how I felt; was me being emotionally abusive & manipulative towards him.

This is not a flowery manuscript filled with empowerment and hope. This is not the life, laugh, love of literature. This story is dangerous because of the truth I have learned through experience, which is that you are damned if you do, damned if you don't. Whatever you choose to do, you will be blamed and condemned for it. There is no right answer to this problem because the entire system is wrong and sets victims up for failure.

This book might not inspire women to leave their abusive husbands. It might instead inspire murder or insight riots. I hope in a way it does because the whole system needs to be burned to the ground to protect those who need to be protected and punish those who have committed real and damaging crimes.

Make no mistake; the physical, emotional and psychological damage that has been caused by my ex-husband's violence and abuse towards me has completely and irrevocably ruined my whole fucking life. And no, for once, I am not being dramatic when I say that. I am probably not being dramatic enough.

I have not written this book to force anyone to believe me. I am at a point in life where I do not fucking care if anyone believes me or not. You can argue with the wall. By writing this book I am stating it is fact and the truth. My real hope in telling my story, owning my truth, is that it will help even one person. This is the book I needed when it was happening to me.

This story is not suitable for anyone who is triggered by anything violent. Contained within this book is a breakdown of what psychological, physical and sexual violence & abuse is. This is a grossly and intentionally over-explained and literal tale of what happened to me at the hands of the man who got down on one knee on Christmas Eve in 2006 and proposed to me. A man who walked down an aisle for me. A man who said confidently with tears in his eyes in front of his friends and family that he would love and honour me for his whole life.

A man that I have spent the last six years hiding from to keep myself and my two children safe.

Introduction

Domestic abuse, domestic violence, intimate partner violence. There are so many terms and ways to talk about this topic and yet, from what I have seen in the media it is still taboo to a point, still reduced and made to seem less than. The emphasis still seems to be on the poor little teddy bear of a man who raped and murdered his wife and how doing such a thing will have a negative impact on his life. Fuck her though, she was obviously a whore and deserved whatever happened to her.

The conversations are around women being a tease, being wild, being too strong or not strong enough. Being prudish, being whorish, being boring or being a slut. We have been blamed for the actions of men as if they are incapable of taking accountability for anything they do.

Women who have in recent decades have become obsessed with true crime because they have been told that when they are raped, kidnapped, murdered that it is their fault. They were not vigilant enough, not physically strong enough, too empathetic, too kind, too available. She should have known better. So, women turned to watching and reading about true crime, studying it and using the knowledge to prevent being attacked in the first place. Living constantly on the edge, always fearful of what someone else will do to us.

This is because we live with the very real threat that men pose.

Now, regarding gender in this book, I am a cis white woman, I would label myself as demisexual and bisexual. As a cis woman, I can only speak on my experience from dating cis men. The emphasis here is on one straight cis man. I am an ally in all issues of gender equality, trans issues and queerness in general regardless of the label. I can only speak from my experience though, this is non-fiction. If you feel I am leaving out any group, it is not because I don't care or don't acknowledge them, it's because I am speaking from my experiences. Domestic abuse and rape can happen to anyone, any age, any gender, any identity, any race, religion or group out there can be impacted and are regularly.

I used to feel extremely alone when I was being abused. I thought that I was the only person in the world that this was happening to. That everyone would look down on me, blame me for it and would not believe me or help me.

I was deeply ashamed of what other people had done to me.

Nothing annoys me more than hearing people ask, "But why didn't you just leave?" It's such a loaded question and there isn't a straightforward answer. There isn't something I can make into a quick and cute little motivational quote because the answer comes from behavioural conditioning. Using fear, an abuser can make someone fearful enough to not leave them, sometimes without ever lifting a hand to that person. That's how powerful manipulation and fear tactics can be.

Not me though, my ex-husband was regularly frustrated at how even after beating me for hours at a time I'd still not be broken enough to just agree with him, like he wanted. It took so much violence to make me cower, to induce a panic attack. My limits for what I can endure are terrible in the worst ways because I was hurt so badly, so often as he kept reminding me simply because I could not do what I was told.

He said to me regularly that I wouldn't get hurt by him as often as I did if I just listened, if I just did what he had told me to. I would try, for a short while anyway but that's a story for a later chapter. We'll get to that. How something fundamental inside of me has always been broken, that danger and fear just didn't make me pause where others would, careful with their words or actions.

I've had people tell me I'm brave and strong for what I've endured, and you know what? I fucking hate that more than anything. All I ever wanted was for someone to save me. Someone to come along and pick me up and take me out of that situation. Even since, I've wanted someone to help me. No one ever did though. I wanted the opportunity to be soft; to be loved and to be loveable and yet, I sit here today probably fuller of anger and wrath than I ever have.

That rage at the injustice of the whole situation has been desensitising. It's a tale about a girl who wanted a love story and instead turned into someone bitter and antisocial. Rage is what gets me out of bed every morning. Wrath is what grits my teeth and makes me put one foot in front of the other to carry myself forward. Spite makes me go about my day when I have wanted nothing more than to curl into my own abyss and stay there. The darkness has become my only friend and confidant.

I'm not brave. I appear and come across brave. I'm actually extremely soft and sensitive.

What I wanted was love, what I got was pain and torture. When I wanted companionship and friendship, I was met with only loneliness, rejection and being disappointed time after time. When I tried to make connections, I was only turned away and left out.

I wish I had a fairytale to spin for you. How I was raped and abused by my first love and after leaving, I became the hottest, wealthiest and best version of myself. How I went on to meet someone new, someone wonderful who restored my faith in love and humanity. I wish I had that fairy tale to tell you today, but this story is only one of pain further endured and strength consistently tested. There is no happy ending except for the silence that I currently write in.

 I'm thirty-nine years old and I have my own home (don't get too excited, it's just a rental from the local council. Technically, that is the equivalent to hitting the jackpot in today's economy). It is peaceful, quiet and there is no shouting or screaming here. No one slams doors or makes you listen out for footsteps so you can act accordingly. I'm listening to Miley Cyrus, no one mocking me for my "shitty" taste in music. I can be myself in peace. I can show emotion, cry without being ridiculed, pointed and laughed at.

 I can paint my walls pink, and I bought two pink sofas for my living room. I don't have to shave my legs if I don't feel like it. I can style my hair however I want. I can also wear whatever clothes I want at home or when/if I go out. I don't have to worry about being called ugly, looked down at and told I'm not good enough.

 I also don't have bruises in strange places anymore. I used to always be covered in bruises and never really knew where they came from. Turns out all those knocks and bangs took their toll.

I can lose weight, gain weight, it's my issue no one else's. I can spend my money however I like. If I overspend, then it's my problem to sort. If I budget well, then great. I can save money, choose to pay back some of the £42,000 debt that was accumulated in my name by my ex-husband. I can buy all the books I want if that's what I choose. I can read whatever I want in peace, no longer needing permission to read romance or explain anything a little smutty. I can cut my hair or grow it out (I haven't yet been brave enough to grow it out properly, the longest my hair has been is chin-length. I've recently shaved my head - I'll explain the significance of hair length later too).

It's a shame because I did really want men to be better than they are. I was rooting for you. I've been a champion for men's mental health my whole life. My biological father (if he is my father at all) was abusive and an addict who viciously abused my mother. My grandfather who raised me, was an alcoholic and dealt with a lot of issues himself.

Maybe it's the neurodivergence, maybe it's just me but I've never understood how or why men and women are viewed differently. I don't believe in hierarchies or societal structures or this notion that men are better than women. Aside from a few simple biological differences, there is no difference. We are all human; we all have access to the full spectrum and range of emotions. Emotions are not a feminine thing. If you've ever been on the receiving end of a man's rage over losing to a video game and throwing their controller across the room or seeing their football team losing, then you know that men are extremely emotional creatures.

Emotions are a human experience; mental illness is also a human experience.

Of course, it's not just men who don't take accountability for their actions or become abusers, we covered that earlier. I am talking from my experiences with people and what I have noticed is that generally those who have been abused, internalise and blame themselves whereas abusers tend to externalise and blame anyone but themselves.

That lack of taking accountability isn't just a "symptom of a mental illness" because anything can be a symptom of a mental illness or neurodivergent condition. It comes down to a person's intent and that then becomes an excuse and manipulative.

You can be mentally ill and be abusive, just like you can be mentally ill and be abused.

The issue becomes being mentally ill and using said illness as an excuse. Yes, the symptoms someone might experience as a mental illness might make them act in an abusive manner, but refusing to take accountability makes a person dangerous to others. AND even worse, the people around them enabling said behaviour and minimising it, gaslighting victims and others. This just creates a cycle of abuse with zero need for the perpetrator to take any accountability. Always knowing they can act how they please and others will fix it for them.

I keep seeing people online talk about overusing the phrase "narcissist" and while I do agree that you can't go around diagnosing other people in general terms, especially since most people do not understand the differences between personality disorders. I absolutely believe without any doubt that there are a huge number of psychopaths and narcissists that live in society more than what they are believed to be. The generalised lack of empathy or selective empathy in the world is a huge red flag and sign of this.

So many people have slipped through the cracks, have evaded detection because we as individuals don't take dangerous people seriously enough. By making excuses for others, by reducing the impact of what crime a person has committed against you or someone else, by denying it, is protecting them. It is enabling them to continue to act that way.

For this reason, I would ask you to seriously consider those abusive people you know. Whether they have been accused but you personally have never experienced that side to them. Really ask yourself if you are in a position to judge them or their victim? Are you the target audience? Or have you been chosen by the abuser to further enable and perpetuate their lies, their mask, their cover of who they truly are? How well do you know anyone, and as such, who are you to judge whether they did what they were accused of?

This is book one of a multi-part series focusing on my very real and for once, honest account of what happened to me when a man took an obsessive interest in me. This first book will focus on the time within the relationship starting with how we met and ending with the day he pushed me so far that I called the police. That was the day he was arrested, July 7th 2019 and was the day I was rescued.

Since then, I have only seen him in court and a few unfortunate incidents where I bumped into him in public places. That is the day I celebrate the end of the relationship. My freedom from being forced to be in a relationship I did not want to be in and was unable to leave by myself.

In later books I will discuss more of what happened within the marriage, and I can for the first time focus on what happened after. This was the whirlwind of police, procurator fiscal, family court, social work, criminal court, him and his family and every trick and loophole he used to harass me, legally for five years until our youngest child turned 16.

Even now editing this book, over six years after his arrest, I am dealing with the fallout of his twisted, manipulative, entitled and downright dangerous actions. I am still struggling to find peace or safety. Perhaps more than ever, I feel at risk.

This is not a fully comprehensive list of every single abusive thing that he did to me.

Every example listed in this book, however, is abusive.

Cast List

For the sake of anonymity & privacy, as this is a non-fiction,

I am changing the names of those involved.

I would like to introduce you to;

The Wife: Louise

The Husband: Allan

My Daughter: daughter

My Son: son

His Mother: Natalie

His Father: Derek

My Mother: Margaret

His Gran: Jennifer

His Grandad: Richard

His Best Friend: Blake

This one is for my now EX-husband

Officially not my problem anymore!

Thank fuck!

And if we burn,

you burn with us!

-Mockingjay, 2010

The beginning, April 2004

The first time I saw him was in poor lighting as he stood at the back of the shop, talking to the manager whom I was there to meet for a job interview. I had only turned eighteen a few weeks before and felt like I was the hottest, most wonderful thing in the whole world.

Self-assured, confident and full of my own ambition and determination, I walked into that little video store that I had been going to since I was a child. It was full of memories, even prior to it being taken over by a large corporation, it had been a video rental store since the 80s. I remember renting my favourite movies like Beetlejuice and The Lion King from there over the years.

We were poor, lower than working class, where we didn't have fresh milk in the fridge or bread in the cupboard at home. All my clothes growing up had been hand-me-downs with holes in them. My mother couldn't afford to have the heating on when it was cold. I didn't even live with her until I turned 15, only spending weekends when she wasn't too tired from working night shifts during the weeks. I lived with her parents; they were abusive and functional alcoholics.

I was a strange child, one obsessed with death and princesses in equal measure. Taking hyper fixations of vampires, old English literature, serial killers, dinosaurs, aliens and the supernatural to the extreme. I was often up trees or riding my bike even though I still had the stabilisers on until I was almost ten years old. I also spent a lot of time in my bedroom at my grandparents alone, or at the library. I took Matilda literally and started going to the library after school by myself and made a mission to read every book in the children's section. The librarians taught me how to order in other books, and this opened the whole world to a child who never knew any real love or kindness.

I was alone, I had been alone my whole life, but I had books and now movies. I would watch films constantly and couldn't afford to go to the cinema, but I could rent them, and I did. I went to college when I left school at 16 and I worked. I liked having money, I liked being able to buy my own things like the books and clothes I wanted. I've always loved shoes and bags. So, this job, when I was considering dropping out of college while studying music meant everything to me.

Allan stood there at the opening of the till that separated the back of the shop for the employees, to the front of the store for the customers. He stood there staring at me and he never took his eyes off me, not as I approached the desk and not as I was led through the back by Michael, the manager.

Allan worked there, had come in on his day off because he wanted to see who was coming in for interviews, he wanted a say. He was only two years older than me, also at college and working there as a part time job, was just a sales assistant himself. This should have been the first red flag because he was clearly pushing his authority in a place where he should have had none.

The interview went well enough, Michael and I talked, and I answered all his questions. The back of the shop was small and left zero impression, same as he did.

I did not get a call until a few weeks later and I did get the impression that I was not Michael's first choice. However, it became increasingly obvious that Allan had pushed so much that I was hired because he bullied Michael into doing so.

This would become a running joke over the years.

My first day there was with Michael, I was to start at 8am and I got myself up, ready and headed off. I made sure to be a little early and as I walked up the slight hill and came over towards the area of the video store sat with a few other small shops. I saw Allan sitting outside the store on a bench. I can still remember that at this moment I was annoyed, I was annoyed at him being here. I can't explain it, but I knew there was something deeply wrong with him.

Now aside, from the intensive staring he had barely interacted with me, we hadn't even spoken up to this point. Yet, something inside of me knew that there was something wrong with him. This is where I began to doubt myself. He hadn't done anything to make me think that and hadn't said anything to make me think such a thing. So, I pushed the thought away, feeling that I was being unfair towards him somehow. I hadn't given him a chance.

This is an important time to note that we do not owe anyone a chance. If your intuition is telling you there is something not right about a person or a place, I would strongly suggest you listen to it. Unfortunately, I have ignored my intuition many times and I can say that every time I did, I was wrong to do so. Trust your intuition, it has never failed me, but I have failed myself by trusting my brain and eyes over what my body knew instinctively straight away.

Creepy, weird and something not quite right with him.

My first real impression of my future husband and the father of my only children.

That was my immediate response to the dark-haired man with equally dark eyes that sat, his body facing away from me, but his head turned around watching me walk towards him. I wasn't expecting to see him there, but something had happened the night before and he was waiting for Michael to arrive.

Turns out that someone had tried to rob the store the night before (I now wonder if this was true at all or staged to give Allan a reason to be there in the morning, knowing it was my very first shift.) while Allan had been on shift and the police were coming to take statements. He wanted to be there to speak to Michael about it and to deal with the police. Apparently, that was something that happened often. It was a rough neighbourhood, the same one my mother had lived in until I was twelve, so I was more than familiar with its reputation. It didn't bother me the way it should.

I got to know him little by little over the next few months and developed a friendship with him. That bond was false and clouded my earlier judgement of this man, who turned out to be the most dangerous person I had ever met and that coming from someone who had grown up around criminals, the mentally ill and addicted.

I knew dangerous men, and women, plenty of them but Allan was a monster worse than any of them. I had been around abusive people my whole life. I thought I knew what it was to be afraid, but Allan taught me something different entirely.

He wore a mask and was extremely good at reading people. I was eighteen and I'd have never admitted it then, but I know now how vulnerable and naive I was. At the time I was still self-harming, seriously restricting my eating and I didn't know I was neurodivergent. Those diagnoses came much later in life. I was struggling, I had been abandoned and neglected by everyone that had ever been in my life.

I was dating a girl who I had dated a few years earlier, but we were both too shy with one another for it to last or develop into anything serious. My previous boyfriend had turned into a stalker who randomly turned up in places and sent me gifts non-stop. I had been raped more than I had consensual sex and yet I blamed myself for those experiences. I didn't have many close friends and was living with my mum in her council flat. I was desperate to make something of myself and improve my life. I was unhealthy skinny with long dark hair, dyed a shade which was called purple black. I wore lots of bracelets to cover the self-harm scars up my wrists and the attempts that I had made in my life.

I was a sad and lonely girl who desperately wanted friends and a partner, a family of my own. I wanted a cute little place to live and dreamed of being a writer. I had been studying music production at college based on a dream of being a singer. I was good at that point; I sang all the time. Over the years, thanks to Allan who said he never understood or liked music that much, I stopped singing and dancing. He slowly turned me away from the little things that made me happy. I had also wanted someone to love me despite my mental illness, someone who tried to understand me and would baby me the way I wanted, felt I needed.

I was also hypersexual. I already had an unhealthy knowledge of BDSM, everything weird and wonderful. I wanted a partner who I could try all these things with and have fun. I knew far too much at far too young an age. At 18 I had wanted to become a porn star and stripper. Confident in my body and self that I was desired by men and that men would want me sexually. Sex I had equated to be the same thing as love, that was a difficult lesson to learn. I had been sexualised since I was a child and that was what had helped me develop an eating disorder that restricted food until I lost the curves that had started to develop with puberty. I deeply rejected my feminine body as a result of the way I had been treated my whole life, aiming for looking a little more androgynous. I was used to being catcalled in public, especially in my school uniform. I know now that I looked even younger than I was, not understanding at the time, that was what made me so appealing to men.

Allan was no different, he was attracted to the "whore" that he, like everyone else, assumed I was but unfortunately for him an incident stopped him from getting what he wanted from me. Always claiming that this incident stopped me from "fully giving myself" to him. Of course, he never created a safe space for me sexually either.

This man ended up turning me off sex and made me feel like a stranger in my own body. Ashamed of myself, my body and of ever wanting anything intimate with anyone.

He played me right from the beginning. Finding out that I liked men who wore pink and other pastel colours, he began dressing that way to impress me. He pretended to have a stutter that he actively faked, because he wanted to come across less intimidating. He was 5ft11 and just as wide in the shoulders, a little chubby but the extra weight didn't look bad on him due to his overall size. He was so broad, he was physically much larger than anyone else who stood beside him.

He pretended to like the same movies and music as I, when he eventually told me he had lied in the first place. I asked him why. "Because you wouldn't have liked me otherwise." He was right, those shared interests at the beginning were what made me feel like we had things in common, that we could spend time and enjoy those things together. The betrayal of him doing this was just one thing amongst many that would fester and grow over the years.

He was not unattractive, but I was not attracted to him. I had a feeling that he was into me. I'm normally not good at telling so he must have been trying to make it obvious for me to have noticed at all. I ignored it and I had no intention of ever getting involved with him like that. I wasn't attracted to him romantically and certainly not sexually.

I now know I am demisexual and I can't imagine myself having sex with anyone. One-night stands don't turn me on; I've never had one. I can only be sexually involved with someone that I have a connection with. It needs to be a cuddly, intimate connection too because I've only ever had sex with someone I've already been in a relationship with (Ok, so it wasn't officially a relationship I was in with that last man HOWEVER, he made me feel like it was) I wouldn't shame anyone else for their preferences but it's a no from me. It doesn't turn me on.

Now, that's how you ruin Christmas!

Allan had spent almost two years convincing me to start hanging out with him. I had refused. Eventually, I got involved with some college filming projects he had been directing during the summertime. Since I didn't want to go out to the clubs or pubs, he had convinced me to start going to the cinema with him. What started off as an outing with a massive group of his friends, over the weeks dwindled down until it was just me & him.

Eventually, a few days before Christmas on the Thursday in 2005, I agreed to go on a night out with him over in the next town. We had agreed to meet at a local pub, The Star, and then get a taxi through to Town.

Walking into the pub with a tiny skirt that barely covered anything and less than £20 in my plastic see through Barbie purse, I was the epitome of, "it's her own fault if it even happened at all." I was a 19-year-old poster child for everything you are told not to do as a woman going out. I didn't care, I genuinely believed I would be in good, safe company and was on track to have an epic night. As it turns out, this night was the one that changed the entire projection of my life and set me down a path I could never have imagined.

Bleached blonde, skinny and blue eyed I always drew attention from people as I passed; arrogant, entitled, spoiled. I had nothing but negatively wonderful things to say about myself. I know now that girl was lonely, scared and desperately needed someone who saw me without the attachment of mental illness or my poorer social standing. I was embarrassed by myself and where I had come from.

Despite all this, I never failed to project confidence as I walked through the pub and found Allan, sitting with his friend at a small table. The other man, Chris, was smaller than Allan but with similar features with equally dark hair and eyes. He had a grin that was hiding something, felt like I had interrupted a private joke that was aimed at me.

"Louise, this is Chris." He smiled at me then, was nice enough but didn't make much of an impression on me.

***

What happened this evening was supposed to just be a fun night out, the first I'd had in a long time. I wasn't a regular drinker or partygoer, as much as he would later suggest. However, when I did go out, I went all out.

That night, I only had £20 on me and had expected Allan to pay for everything. He had been paying for everything for the last six months when we went to the cinema, it was normal. It meant that because he wasn't buying my drinks, I wasn't drinking much. I had one Bacardi Breezer at that first bar before we got in the taxi to Town. Then I had one Smirnoff Ice when we went to the first bar when we got there. Upon entering the nightclub, he took me to the VIP section, and I was given a glass of champagne. I only had a few sips.

That is the drink I believe was spiked.

It was too little alcohol spaced over a few hours to cause what happened next.

I blacked in and out, the next thing I was dancing in the middle of the dancefloor, I was surrounded by men. I saw Allan watching me from the side, he looked disgusted.

Then I remember throwing up all over a table in the back, and yes, I also threw up on the people who were sitting there.

Sometime later I was aware again and was being pressed against a barrier and was raped. In the middle of the club, which was now loud, dark and packed full of people. I cried, I don't know who it was or what the person looked like aside from they were much taller and bigger than me.

I blacked out again and I don't know what happened because next I was aware, I was standing in the middle of the dancefloor looking around for someone, anyone I knew. I found someone I knew from college, Benjamin, who I had seen recently, having interviewed his band at a gig about a month prior. We spoke online sometimes, I was due to help Allan film his band's live performance a few days later at a different pub there in Town. He looked at me, also in disgust, that look of what the fuck is wrong with her. He laughed at me for being with someone who was "fat & ugly," his words. The only description I have of my rapist.

I asked him to help me. I think he said he was going to find someone.

A little later, I was stumbling around and crying, upset and trying to figure out what was happening to me. I stood in the middle of the dancefloor and just let out a loud scream. I was desperate for someone to notice me, to help me.

What happened instead was a bouncer came up behind me, startling the ever living fuck out of me and grabbed me around the waist. The pain was excruciating. I had bruises afterwards. He picked me up, and took me outside, dumping me on the pavement. Allan had followed. I heard talk of, "She's too drunk, I'm not letting her back in."

I had wanted help, and he had further traumatised me and hurt me.

Allan had managed to negotiate with them, as he knew them all from being a regular, to get my bag and phone which had been left behind. They did thankfully.

Later he'd tell me that he had rescued me again this evening as someone, having seen me dumped outside the club, tried to get me into a taxi with them. He had intervened, stopping them and me being hurt again, worse probably. Did that happen? I don't know.

***

Raped and afraid, terrified to face the reality of what had happened earlier that evening I proved to him once and for all that I was the perfect victim, the perfect wife and the perfect accessory to all the evil he wished to achieve. He told me to go to the police, but I refused. He told me to go to the hospital, I refused. He offered to go with me, I refused.

Allan had me exactly where he wanted me. I refused to go because reporting it to the police would have made it real. I would have been forced to accept that what happened had happened. Pushing it away, helping me forget would save my mental health in the moment. Long term, the trauma never left, until Allan gave me so much himself, that it took over my brain and was forced down with everything else. It destroyed me.

I realised later in life, the reason it had such a devastating impact on me is because every other time I have been raped or sexually assaulted, it had been a friend, family member, boyfriend, partner, husband. This had been a stranger, somehow that felt worse, like I couldn't gaslight myself into believing it was my fault. I had to acknowledge it was rape, I had been raped. I had managed to deny myself or blame myself for other people's actions. I protected the ones I knew well & cared for, but a stranger? It forced me to see rape for what it was, and it destroyed me.

The so-called party girl stopped going out.

I stopped drinking alcohol for years.

Everything hurts. I've always been haunted by fierce emotions, running wild inside of me, always fighting to burst out. He is the only person who has ever been capable of making me lose control. How easy he manipulated me; how easy it must have been to read me and push all the right buttons. He knew exactly what to say or even just how to look at me for those overwhelming emotions to burst out. I was reactive, always taking what he gave me and multiplying it.

That night Allan learned a lot about me. My refusal to involve the police despite them most likely being security camera footage to back up my story, and witnesses to corroborate what happened to me. He learned that I would not involve the police at any cost. My refusal to go to the hospital also gave him confirmation that I was not the type to seek help even when I really needed it.

In those two acts of saying no, I confirmed to him what he surely knew already, why he had targeted me in the first place; that I would be the perfect victim for him. Someone who no matter how mouthy I could be, would never speak to the police. Someone he could manipulate and abuse, create the perfect cover for what he wanted most of all.

What he did next though is what solidified in my mind that he would be the perfect partner for me. He came with me when I went to the pharmacist to get tested for STI's and pregnancy. He wrapped me up, literally in his duvet and looked after me. I spent the next two weeks going to his parents' house and spending the day in his bedroom (not like that, I had been raped, and he was at this point, acting like a perfect gentleman. Someone who seemed to know what empathy was).

He wrapped me in his duvet where I either sat on the floor or on his bed, and he kept me fed (I was better fed by him than I had been in my own home. The extreme skinniness I had shrunk to, started to fill me out a little more in my jeans. This originally had me panicking) and put on movies for me. He always chose ones he thought I'd like, and the bastard had the innate talent at picking things I ended up loving.

To this day he is still responsible for introducing me to what became my all-time favourite books and movies.

I wasn't thinking about love or boyfriends or sex, not at that point in life. I was traumatised by what had happened to me. It wasn't the first time I had been raped, hardly, but this had such a devastating impact on me.

I did start to see him in a different light though, I started wondering if this was what a real relationship was and would be like. How being loved by someone who I genuinely thought loved me, liked me for who I was, and wanted me, would be. Is this how it's supposed to be? Allan made me feel safe, gave me a place by his side when he had a huge group of friends and people around him. Yet he was always chasing after me. I felt special, he made me feel special. Not just because I was pretty, he made me feel listened to, liked and seen.

I thought it was real.

I had met his parents, his grandparents, his friends; everyone loved him and spoke highly of him. Everyone liked him, and I had no one, I was barely liked, only tolerated and even my family couldn't be bothered with me. Not like him, they all spent time together, had meals and parties and he was always out doing something with someone.

He always made time for me.

He had laughed at me when I told him I had never tried Chinese food before, so he took me to a local Chinese buffet restaurant. This became our place as he later proposed to me here. He always paid for everything and he had me trying new foods. He had me experiencing a life I never had, and despite making fun of me for it, I just thought that was banter. It was a little later before he started openly displaying how much he looked down on me for my humble roots.

How he felt I wasn't good enough for him.

A new life

I had been at college studying communication, at the time my dream was to work as a music journalist as my day job and write novels in my spare time. That's what I felt would help me reach my goal of being a full-time novelist.

I had been groomed for university since I was a child, my grandad wanted me to get an education because I'd be the first in the family to do so. He had me sit for hours and memorise the dictionary as a child to make sure I had a good vocabulary. I hadn't thought about applying, I had missed the cut off time for applications starting September 2006.

I did help Allan with his application for uni. He had one university in mind; he was only applying there and nowhere else. One night while chatting online with one another about it, I decided fuck it and applied myself. His was down in London and honestly, I was worried about him going all that way. I knew it would be the end of the relationship, and I had gotten quite attached to him. I had expectations at this early stage due to his excessive love bombing. He practically spent every waking moment with me, or at the very least, on the phone to me.

I decided that studying English would be best for me as I wanted to be an author and three universities in Scotland had this course; Glasgow, St Andrews and Dundee (not Abertay). At 1am I threw together an application with a written statement, paid the fee to UCAS and hit send.

Despite missing the January cut off time, I was offered an unconditional place at all three universities. I had my pick. I decided that Glasgow was too far away, and I wasn't brave enough at that point. St Andrews despite being the one I wanted, the most prestigious, was too close. It was in Fife, and I wanted out of Fife as a bare minimum. Prince William had graduated from St. Andrews the previous year in 2005. So, I chose Dundee University and started looking into moving into the dorms.

Allan did not get selected for Ravensbourne University. He received his rejection around the same time I received my acceptances. He also found out that a female classmate of his had been accepted in what he considered his place. He hid it well at the time, but this resentment festered and bred so much hatred towards me later.

DUNDEE

JULY 2006 – DECEMBER 2006

Excited for my life to begin!

A lot of things happened in very quick succession. After we talked about the fact that I would be going to Uni, he now had no plans having graduated college and no longer had another option with university. We decided to move to Dundee together, getting a flat so that I could study and he would get a job.

We looked for a flat together, after all, this is something that his friend had done with his girlfriend and had worked well for them. As a result, we ended up with a beautiful two-bedroom flat along Baffin Street, close to where Mary Shelley once lived. There was a sign stating this, I would go and look at it. I remember reading Frankenstein while sprawled out on the two-seater sofa we had under the massive bay windows. It was all rather gothic and romantic to me. I thought about how she had been younger than me when writing such an influential book, but I would now be able to write my own stories properly.

I am in no way comparing myself to Mary Shelley or anything I've written to Frankenstein, however, it felt fated as if I was in the right place. I was inspired; I was in love with life, possibilities and Dundee felt like home. It felt right, for the first time in my life, I felt like I was exactly where I was supposed to be. That wonderful things could and would happen.

I had been in Dundee again in 2021/2022 when I dated that other abusive man, I realised then how far my flat had been from the university. I was used to walking, we never had a car and couldn't afford public transport. How isolated his choice of flats was, keeping so far away from everyone I could possibly meet at university. As it was between studying, my job and Allan, I never had time to attend a single night out, party or make any friends. The one girl I did meet who seemed nice and excited to talk to me, I ended up being too busy to make any real connection with her or anyone else.

I also had an internet friend at this time; someone I had been chatting with online for years. She was a year older than me; we had bonded over music and literature through Live Journal. Her name was Shelley. We had exchanged addresses and had been sending each other Christmas presents for a few years. When he found out I had given her the address of the flat, he went mental at me; shouting & screaming at me. He told me that I wasn't allowed any money in our budget to buy her a gift, something I'd managed previously no matter how little money I'd had previously. Another connection due to him I wasn't able to maintain and ultimately lost.

I was left in the flat the first few weeks. He would take the key as there was only one, saying that it was against the tenancy agreement to have a second key cut. I couldn't see how it would matter. Instead, I was usually locked inside the flat when he left for work. I could get out in an emergency, there was a snib on the lock, but I wouldn't have been able to secure the flat to go anywhere or get back inside. I once had to get the downstairs neighbour to drive me to Allan's workplace to get the key from him, when I accidentally locked myself out putting rubbish in the communal bins round the back.

I was used to being isolated; it never felt like the red flag it is. Looking back, I can see how trapped I had been by him. He bought me books to read, with my money as everything went into his bank account because he told me it was easier for paying the direct debits. He bought me my own copies of Buffy the Vampire Slayer TV show because I wanted to watch it, it was his favourite TV show. He didn't trust me touching his DVDs, so he bought me my own set.

My ex-boyfriend from when I was 16, had started calling me again. It pissed Allan off despite my pleas that I had tried to tell him not to, that I didn't want to speak to him. Billy wouldn't listen. Eventually after a few months, it was Allan who picked up the phone, spoke to him and spooked him enough that he never contacted me again.

That was the last time I ever spoke to him but Allan would bring him up constantly even up to the months prior to his arrest; jealous that I had been with anyone before him.

When I did start university properly, I was excited and wanted to get involved in everything! I'd excitedly go back to him and talk about the classes, lectures, the study groups. It was everything I ever wanted it to be, but I never got enough of it. I wanted to be in the middle of all the education but that wasn't possible. With Allan taking up my time, my part time job that ended up being 40+ hours a week and taking on board all the chores including the cooking, it was too much for me to focus. I still managed; I wasn't about to give up.

Allan was convinced that I was having an affair with every professor I encountered. Anyone I mentioned from the study groups; I was having sex with them according to him. I tried to explain that wasn't true and he wouldn't listen. He had convinced himself that I was cheating on him. I wasn't. He also never let me meet with the landlord alone, who insisted on in person, cash payments every month, as he was convinced I'd have sex with the man.

It became exhausting very quickly.

Another major event that happened early on was within two weeks of university starting, my grandad died. He passed away in the toilets at the local hospital while waiting for a routine appointment. He never kept well, so it wasn't a huge surprise. I had been expecting him to die since I was young, as he always talked about it. My grandad raised me. He referred to me as his daughter. His death was perhaps the only one that affected me. Allan and I went back for the funeral. It was tense. My mother sat me next to the coffin out of spite.

I knew that if my grandad had been alive when Allan first physically assaulted me, he would never have been able to do so a second time.

It's just a joke!

Picking up the call, which was the constant telephone communication that I had with him when he was physically not in my presence, I was listening to him tell me about his day. He had just left work, was at the bus stop and waiting for the bus that would take him home to me. As usual it was rapid fire, being overwhelmed by the constant stream of ideas that he was jumping back and forth from. I had noticed that when he was telling me things it was hard to keep track because he would change mid-way and jump onto something else. He also had a terrible habit of starting a sentence in the middle, not at the beginning. I struggled to keep up and it was difficult to understand what he was talking about sometimes. He would get angry when I couldn't understand what he was saying.

    Back to my wonderful boyfriend, the man I was proud to call my own for a while but a much shorter while than we were together. He was chatting away and as I wandered around the flat, mostly listening to him, there was suddenly an almighty crash and bang at the front door, and I froze. There was someone trying to break in! I immediately told Allan, and he told me to get away from the door, to hide. I started crying as the banging and kicking continued, just waiting for the door to come off the hinges. It was relentless as I stood there stuck in place, crying on the phone to him begging him to come home, to save me, protect me. I didn't know what to do and through it all, the only part of what he said that still stays with me today was, "Louise, I've only just gotten on the bus, I'll not be home for another 25 minutes."

The terror was coursing through me, nailing my feet to the floor, unable to move, to turn around, to run or hide like he kept suggesting. A new wave of tears every time there was a bang at the door. I screamed after a particularly loud kick that reverberated through the flat, a noise that I felt underneath my skin, deep in my bones. I was shaking, crying and begging him to come home. I was terrified of what was about to happen. How that door was going to come in, either split in two or completely ripped from the hinges. How men, possibly two judging from the noise, were going to come in, with who knows what intentions, but they would see me standing there and they would hurt me. How convinced I was that they would hurt me and how much more scared I became at the thought.

I already knew what violence men were capable of. I already knew what might happen to me, how I'd be unable to protect myself and how I'd have to wait, to endure and hope that Allan made it home in time, before damage was irreversible.

Finally, as my whole body was preparing for the worst that could happen, the banging outside stopped completely and it was Allan's voice that I heard, not on the telephone I was holding, squeezing, as if holding it would protect me but outside the door.

I was too scared to react properly, he called to me through the door, and I opened it up. It had been him all along. He later told me he got away from work earlier than normal and had wanted to play a prank on me.

Another time he was coming home from work, speaking to me on his mobile and tried to joke about being hit by a car. After a few moments of silence, he put on a fake foreign accent and pretended to be a by-stander who had witnessed the accident. This person was trying to tell me that the man who had been talking to me on the phone was in fact lying dead in the street. He spent a good amount of time trying to convince me that Allan was dead, pushing me to believe it.

Of course, he'd say later, it was just a joke. This was something he did regularly and to different degrees. Sometimes he'd tell me he'd gotten a job offshore that meant he would have to leave for six months at a time, just to make me upset and cry that he would be leaving, knowing I'd miss him (at the time I would have). He was known for playing pranks on people. He wasn't; however, someone who could take a joke being made at his expense.

Moving too fast

I remember sitting on his knee on the sofa in the spare room and him coming out with, completely out of the blue, "We should have a baby." I was completely frozen because what do you mean a baby? A baby was not part of my ten-year plan. I was only just getting used to being at university and was enjoying it massively. I love education. I would have happily stayed in further education (not school because I had an awful time being bullied by people) and learning anything and everything.

The plan mainly consisted of establishing a career and making MONEY. Not just money but MONEY. I wanted to live a life that wasn't just comfortable but luxurious. I believed that with education, a good solid work ethic, and hard work I could achieve that. I never expected to be handed it, I never came from money, but I did think I could work for it and earn it.

Then, perhaps when I was financially stable, I could think about having a child. One child specifically because I was an only child and truly believed that no matter how lonely I had been, it was better having just one.

"A baby?"

He had already talked about marriage; we were living together. It was difficult because I was at university and working 40+ hours a week, fully taking care of myself, all the cooking and household chores. He was only working a standard 40-hour job weekly with no other responsibilities. I was the one managing the finances and bringing in more money than he was. I was doing everything, but I was already used to being the one doing everything.

I had told him I was scared about having children and them being abused the way I had been. My best idea to stop this from happening was not having children at all. I told him about all my anxieties and fears surrounding kids and family. He listened and he agreed with me. Made me feel listened to and heard.

He agreed with me that we would have a baby and stay in Dundee so that I could continue at Uni, because that was an investment into our future together as a family. He agreed that we wouldn't use family to babysit, that if we had a child, we would raise the child ourselves. He told me everything I wanted to hear, and I agreed. With his encouragement I stopped taking birth control to try since there was no way I would get pregnant quickly. It never happened straight away, right?

Wrong. Unfortunately for me, I always fall pregnant extremely quickly and found out I was four weeks pregnant on December 4th 2006. I was unbelievably happy, but I was also scared. This was a huge deal, but I had so many fears around what could go wrong with the pregnancy. I was so happy though. At that moment I believed that we were building our family, that I had a supportive, caring man who wanted this family with me as much as I did.

Almost as soon as the doctor confirmed the pregnancy, he broke the one-year lease on our flat behind my back with the landlord. He had his gran organise a rental home back in Hometown, just doors away from her with one of her friends who was a landlord. He put in his notice at his job and got in touch with his friend's mum about getting a job with her back home.

The rug was pulled out from underneath my feet. He never spoke to me about doing these things. He did them and then told me when it was confirmed. I argued against him, but I felt fragile. I was scared that too much stress would cause a miscarriage. I tried to keep my stress levels down and not get wound up by him betraying my trust. He told me he knew better, he would take care of me, but we needed to be around family.

I didn't want to be, not because I'm petulant as everyone would say but because they weren't safe to be around least of all with a child, a baby. There was something about his family that made me feel detached from them. They seemed so nice, so normal, welcoming and yet it didn't feel that way.

I felt trapped. I felt broken and I felt alone. I was twenty years old; I had no one on my side to help fight my battles with me or even encourage me that I was right for having a different opinion. I didn't feel confident enough on my own. I had to trust that he did know better that maybe I was wrong, or overreacting. Was I being dramatic? That's what everyone always said. Crazy, that's what they also called me. Was I? Was I the problem?

I let him lead. I let him make decisions for us that I didn't feel I had any choice in, no voice of my own. I didn't think I could be on my own with a baby. I didn't know what else to do but follow him back to the one place I had spent my whole life trying to run away from.

I was overjoyed and happy to be pregnant. A soon to be massive belly filled with a beautiful baby girl and endless possibilities. So happy to start a family and begin my life. Nothing in my life compares to that time where my belly grew and the movements inside kept me entertained for hours. Seeing her (or later his) little foot or hand push up on my large belly was a beautiful sight and one that was far too short lived. I wish I could have experienced that again, in an environment where I was safe and protected. Able to just enjoy being pregnant.

For eleven years I had been anorexic, only realising the necessity to eat upon learning this wonderful news and having another life to become healthy for, I ate. I ate well but only moved up one dress size going from an 8 to a 10. There had always been something youthful looking about me, seemingly more of a child than I was even aware of, at that age I thought I knew everything, but I admit now I was far too young to become a mother. I was inexperienced in life and not stable enough on my own to have coped without Allan at that time. He had me trapped immediately, now needing him more than I felt comfortable with.

BACK HOME

THE PRIVATE LET

JANUARY 2007 – NOVEMBER 2007

THAT fucking job

Of course, leaving Dundee meant I also had to leave my job. I argued with him endlessly about staying at university, but it was hard traveling back and forth by bus. I started to miss lectures and study groups because it became impossible to be in Dundee and attend all the ones that I needed while living so far away. My grades didn't slip much but even handing in my work on time became trickier. Pregnancy is difficult and I remember almost shitting myself twice on the bus due to intestinal issues. This was extremely embarrassing for me at the time, and my anxiety spiralled as a result.

Without my job, he didn't have as much money coming in as he liked. He was earning the same, but he always wanted more. Originally when we moved, he had told me not to worry about working, since that was one of the many lies and ways he had tried to manipulate me into compliance with the move. That I could concentrate on studying and our baby. I felt pressured into getting some kind of job though, he made me feel bad about not working. Always saying one thing, then switching up and saying the opposite. I could never keep up with him.

I ended up getting hired at a local telephone sales job for a large company. They had a small office on the outskirts of town, difficult to get to without a car. At the time, I believed that sitting at a desk and talking to customers on the phone would be easy, or at least, an easier option than most jobs available.

I was wrong.

What I entered was a hellhole of bullying & gaslighting. The job paid better than it should have, something that would later be a reason why the site was closed. Even now thinking about it, I feel pushed to be positive in the same way abuse trains you to be. It wasn't all bad though; there were some good people I met, one who started at the same time I did. She was a beacon of hope in an otherwise depression inducing workplace. She was the only real friend I ever had. The only person who stuck up for me. But after all those years, I felt like I wasn't good enough to be her friend.

Is he trying to make me have a mental breakdown?

His Batchelor party was a massive multi-day event that started in our hometown, and had minibuses that took the huge group of his friends and family to Dundee. There they did Lazer tag, bowling and went crawling from one pub and club to another. They visited strippers and Allan was stripped down to his bare arse. I was told that he was spanked with a belt by two beautiful women in front of everyone for being the one getting married.

If I had done that, or anything similar I would have been in so much trouble.

I was massively pregnant and didn't want to do anything because he had managed to alienate me from anyone I did have left. My male friends he didn't trust, he never allowed me to go anywhere or do anything without him. I had no opportunity to meet anyone new or to make new friends.

Instead, I got a meal with his female family members for my Bachelorette party, and Michael's then girlfriend Lauren. She and I had started to get a little close, we could have been friends. This caused an issue with one of his friend's wives, Jessie, as she felt entitled to come to any party I had. It wasn't my choice, and I hadn't arranged it. I tried to explain that to her and she didn't seem to understand.

Jessie was an interesting one because she was labelled "crazy" and "a whore" not just by Allan, but everyone in their friendship group. She had apparently been cheating on her soon to be husband, Marcus, with everyone; neighbours, his own brother etc to the point that their wedding was shortly after ours and Allan refused to be the best man. Now, she had apparently tried to have sex with Allan a few times when she was drunk. Both before him and I dated and on the night before my wedding.

There was an interesting incident at a local nightclub prior to when I met him. She had been flirting with someone, dancing with them while the three of them; Jessie, Marcus & Allan had been out together one night. They were all drunk but Marcus chose to ignore his then girlfriend's behaviour. It was Allan who stepped up to defend her and his friend's honour. He took the guy outside and beat the living hell out of him. According to Allan, both Marcus and Jessie were shocked at the difference in what they saw in him that night.

He frequently went on about how many fights he had gotten into before he turned 18. This incident, after he had turned 18, had made him become more careful knowing he'd risk trouble with the police. His father was a policeman, and spent his career becoming more and more respected in his role. I couldn't remember the name of this guy to tell the police when I was interviewed and asked about previous violent incidents that Allan had.

Were him and Jessie fucking the whole time?

I thought he was defending his friends, was he really just an opportunist?

She was always messaging him, and later he would show me these messages saying that he didn't do anything to encourage her. Considering how he talks about me to others, I do wonder if they were having an affair. I wonder if her daughter, born before I started dating Allan, is Allan's biological child.

I also wonder if he is the biological father of any of his female best friend Sarah's four children. I had a feeling something was going on, every time I said anything to him about any of the women he was close with, he gaslit me. His lies have always been so convincing that I did believe him when he said he hadn't cheated, that he would never cheat on me.

There's also Polly...

He made a fool of me, so much was done behind my back right from the beginning, I barely saw or understood it. Spending so much time just trying to hold on and survive one attack to the other left me unable to pay attention to what else was going on around me.

Then there's the one person I don't have the guts to ask about...

Looking back, I think something similar happened to Lauren with Michael as it did with Allan and I, her mood was frequently down. She had upped and left one day with very little warning, going back home to England. They had met online, and she had moved up here to live with him.

We tried to keep in touch but over time that fizzled out.

***

I will never forget being woken up constantly to that fucking buzzer going off. It was the season finale of Lost. He had Michael (who would later enjoy telling us about how many hours he'd spent on the darknet) download the episodes as they aired in America before they did here in the UK. Of course Allan had to see it before everyone else, no one was allowed to spoil anything for him. Staying up until 3am most days, he would watch TV in bed next to me, for my benefit apparently, so I wasn't lonely.

He would have usually sat downstairs, even falling asleep on the couch after watching hours of television; TV shows & movies. The absolute selfish asshole couldn't watch tv unless the surround sound was connected. The volume had to be loud so he could have a full cinematic experience whether downstairs in the living room or upstairs in the bedroom.

This, the lack of sleep and being pregnant at the time drove me insane. I lost the ability to think rationally. That FUCKING BUZZER OR BELL OR ALARM OR WHATEVER THE FUCK IT WAS seemed to be going off every few minutes for what felt like the whole hour long or 40-minute episode.

The absolute fucking rage I felt.

It felt like never once did it occur to him to put it off or even turn it down.

He knew though, I felt like he couldn't possibly understand what he was doing to me otherwise he wouldn't do it. That's never the case with things like this. These are deliberate tactics to cause mental deterioration. Abusers know exactly what they are doing, this was intentional as all his behaviour was.

Eventually after he spent weeks doing this with one TV show or movie or another, I went off sick from work due to stress and depression. I was miserable, I was exhausted, and I felt terrible physically, mentally and emotionally. He was not helping with the chores around the house and still expecting sex multiple times a day. I felt pressured by everything and unable to cope with any of it.

I went to the doctors without speaking to Allan, the GP agreed signing me off was best for mine and the baby's health. I remember being downtown when I had phoned him to tell him, he screamed at me on the phone.

He disappeared for a while, saying he had gone to speak to his grandad for advice. I believed him. He told me that he didn't know if he would come home. I panicked. I didn't want to be alone. I wanted my fiancé, my soon to be husband to support me and care about my health.

Eventually he came home and told me that his grandad had told him he should call off the wedding. That his grandad was disappointed in me. It hurt me to hear that. I cared about his grandparents, I had wanted to be accepted and loved by them. I begged him not to call off the wedding.

The night before the wedding

The night before the wedding I spent the evening at my mum's so that I could get ready in tradition. He was at our home where I wanted to be. I had no regard for tradition and my anxiety was already tightly bound in needing him, having to be around him. As much as I loved being away and having peace to myself, back in my old bedroom I wanted to be at home in my own bed. I also knew I was missing the party he was having. I innocently believed that he was just having fun with friends, I never thought for one second I had anything to worry about. This would just be a continuation of the second, separate life that he inevitably led away from me.

    The night before the wedding I had said how much I wanted to be at home, sleeping in my own bedroom and getting ready where all my stuff was. He said no.

    He wanted the house to himself; he had his friends coming over and they had a party planned for him. I said I could go to the party too but he said no. That it was tradition not to see each other the night before the wedding.

I said fuck tradition because I genuinely didn't care, and I was heavily pregnant and somehow, he had convinced me to stay overnight at my mum's. Now what you need to know is that she had pretty much disappeared at this point, had barely been speaking to me, she never even gave out my wedding invites to family like I had asked her to.

Somehow, even though I did not want to go and spend the night there, he managed to convince me it was for the best.

I think this is a great example of how convincing he was and how even then, I felt unable to say no because I am someone, especially at 32 weeks pregnant, who would rather cut off their own dominant hand than stay over at anyone else's house, especially my mother's.

I texted him a few times, tried to call and he never answered me, barely replied to any messages. I felt alone, I had been abandoned and could not shake the feeling that something was wrong.

The Wedding

The day started alone. My mother, despite physically being there, was not involved with anything to do with my wedding. Thinking back now, she did nothing to even celebrate the fact that her only child was getting married. No decorations, nothing special at all. We went to my gran's, my grandad now dead, knowing how much she hated me, and condemned me getting married at all. She had been the one after all who had called me a disappointment and said she was glad my grandfather was dead, so he didn't have to see the shame of me getting married and being pregnant. She told me so on the phone when I had announced I was pregnant earlier in the year.

    I bathed by myself; I dressed and did my makeup and hair by myself in my old bedroom. It was a horrible experience. I didn't have any friends of my own, no family that clearly cared about me. The only genuinely nice moment that morning came from the aunt that I barely knew, Helen, who gave me her diamond necklace to borrow. With my £180 wedding dress I had bought online & my fake flowers from Ebay, it was too much and yet not enough. I felt like I deserved more, that being pregnant and getting married I deserved some love and celebration and yet there was none.

I knew then that I was nothing to my family and as such, they were nothing to me.

Their complete lack of feeling towards me made me vow that the man I was marrying was my only family, all the family I would ever need. And as such, Allan had to do little to isolate me from them, just agree with my decision and watch my world implode.

The next time I would stay over at my mum's would be the day that he was arrested and I had to leave with two kids, four dogs and myself as my own precious bought home was sealed off by forensics.

***

The uncle I barely knew walked me down the aisle by my gran's request as it's "what my grandad would have wanted." Yet after the awful things she had said about me, I was almost ready to tell them all to fuck off, not to attend since no one clearly wanted to be there and just walk down the aisle by myself.

I realised I wasn't a traditional person and didn't want the things that others did. I was angry by the traditions that stated I should have family at my wedding who did not support me, love me or even like me.

Why should they get to dictate what I did or who should be at my own wedding?

I was done listening to any of them and held my vow in my heart that I would never actively seek them out again.

***

Walking down the aisle, anxiety roared at me to stop, to turn and run away. Little did I know I'd spend the rest of my life being someone who runs due to the decision at that moment to stay. I shook my brazen head, full of life and the arrogance of hope. Telling myself quietly but if it doesn't work out, I can just divorce him.

Silly, naive and impressionable I was a dreamer, a hopeless romantic who believed that life could really be beautiful once it was lived, really lived, present and accountable for one's own self and ambition. I found myself at the bottom of the aisle desperately realising I did not know what I was doing. I was sacrificing my innocence, my youth and everything I was to marry this man.

Allan cried as I walked down the aisle, and his friend Blake had to hold him up and in place as I walked closer to him.

Divorce would be an option if things took a bad turn, I tried to reassure myself.

Turns out that, divorce would never be an option. This man was in it for the long run. Anyone else would have believed him to be a good man, that I was truly lucky to have caught one so good.

I felt sore and tired from the pregnancy, 32 weeks and counting, approaching her due date and excited but also cautious, a warning slowly, quietly beginning in my mind. His behaviour had changed a little and I had seen a side to him that worried me. Everyone gets stressed though, he had a lot going on and was still young himself, only twenty-three to my twenty-one. We were just babies with all the time in the world to grow and learn, to become secure and responsible adults, productive and people that others would be proud of.

Pretty little idiot.

I don't remember much about us exchanging vows except feeling extremely nervous about being in front of a lot of people, most of whom I didn't even know, especially not well. I knew I had no one in that crowd who was there for me. I was completely alone except I was aligning myself with what I thought was a good man, someone who would look after me and protect me. What I didn't realise at the time, was he was the one who I would need to be protected from.

Nothing at the wedding was my choice; not the date, the venue, the food or the cake. I never had a piece of my own wedding cake. I could barely eat the meal because of my pregnancy cravings were more a list of foods that made me want to be violently sick.

Thankfully the men in his family, his dad and grandad specifically kept making sure I had plenty of fluids because I was thirsty and had no money of my own. Allan certainly wasn't looking after me and had refused to buy me separate food, stating that there was plenty here to eat already.

If you don't know what it's like being pregnant, I can tell you that at 32 weeks, I was and felt huge. I am five foot four inches and up until then I had been anorexic, I was skinny and underweight, had been for years. I'm lucky I even got pregnant. I wasn't used to carrying excess weight or navigating the world with a large tummy.

I was terrified I'd slip or fall. It's uncomfortable to stand, and just as uncomfortable to sit down. Especially in chairs in a bar. Jokes were made about me ordering pizza to the wedding venue. I was first to leave the evening celebration, we did go and get Domino's pizza because I had barely eaten.

Being pregnant is hard work, the extra weight, the nervousness around always protecting my belly, counting the number of times she moved or the time in between when she didn't. My anxiety might have been brewing underneath the surface, but it exploded into action when I was pregnant because I was terrified I would lose the baby.

Being at a wedding, least of all the centre of attention was the worst while having to stand, having to dance, having to move around and be uncomfortably sober amongst everyone who was drunk.

Anytime I tried to explain to anyone about how unhappy and uncomfortable I had been at my wedding; I was told I was selfish.

After all the pictures and meals one of my clear memories of the wedding was standing at the far side of the dance floor with Allan beside me. He was looking across the hall at the door, waiting for people to arrive. It was seven o'clock and all the guests would be arriving for the evening part of the wedding. Since his parents had paid for the wedding to be held here, they had filled up the seating at the wedding and meal with all their friends and family. I had to fight for the few members of my own family and as such, Allan only managed a few of his friends who he had battled with his parents about them being allowed to attend the day part.

I was told I was selfish at arguing at all, that I should be grateful that they had paid for it despite it not being what I wanted, and I never asked them to.

As such, most of his friends were invited to the evening and I had no one to invite anyway. As his friends arrived, bursting through into the hall like the idiots they all were, he turned to me, told me he had been bored spending so much time with me and walked away from me. Leaving me standing there on my own without anyone to go sit with.

I remember looking around, my hand on my huge belly, feeling near tears because I was embarrassed. I had no one to go sit with, no one who I could spend the evening with. I was alone. I would say that I have never felt as alone as I did in that moment but that was just the introduction to what my marriage would be.

I had spent my whole life alone, shunned and neglected, a bother to anyone who was supposed to look after me, love me. As such I had a desire to be loved as an adult, thinking I had found my person, yet again, he was starting to show me who he really was underneath all those smiles and nice words. I hadn't yet seen the monster, not really, that would come soon after.

I walked away to the corner and sat by myself in the dark at my own wedding.

***

When we got the photographs back after the wedding, one of the first things my mum said to me was how fat I looked. And I wonder where I got my eating disorder from.

I don't feel ungrateful, I feel let down and manipulated by people I wanted to please. It was important to me that not having any family I could rely on myself that his family liked me. In the end they never liked me at all, barely tolerating me. But they, like Allan, took advantage of me and manipulated me using my impressionable nature and need to please. All I wanted was a real family, a happy one that was supportive and loving. I wanted all the things I had never had. Was it too much to ask and hope for?

Barely married one month and the shit hits the fan

The first time he physically hurt me was in the time frame between getting married on June 24th 2007 and having my daughter 12 days after she was due, in August 2007 after being induced at hospital. I believe it was in July, but it may have been August. Doesn't really matter. The point is I was 32 weeks pregnant at the wedding and super anxious, having nightmares about her dying and constantly checking on her because she didn't move about much on a good day.

I was constantly back and forth to the hospital and laughed off by the midwives for being a silly little girl. I can't help that I've always looked younger than I am but that doesn't mean my concerns weren't valid or worth checking. I had real fears and felt like no one was taking me seriously. Again, another reason I would later struggle to reach out to others and ask for help.

One day he grabbed me by the throat and pinned me to the cupboard that housed the fridge/freezer. My feet were off the ground. I was terrified. He was screaming at me. I wet myself.

He walked off as if nothing happened. He made no mention of it afterwards and I was too scared to. Too scared and ashamed and honestly, I couldn't believe it had happened.

My brain could not comprehend that he had done that. Yes, he was jealous and possessive and tore me down for the silly things I liked to wear but physically violent towards me? He had a very firm grip on whatever temper he was hiding because I could not believe he had done that, especially to me.

What had happened, you may ask for him to respond like that? It's incredibly simple and feels ridiculous to me to even talk about it. It was such a silly thing and yet, it set him off in a way I had been yet to experience with him.

He had been at his gran's, a few doors down from where we lived and had phoned me. I answered the call, listened to him tell me all about this competition that was going on currently on some radio station. For some reason he couldn't call the radio station himself from his gran's.

Now, I'm not sure if I questioned this at the time. His grandparents had a landline, they both had mobile phones, and he was currently phoning me on his mobile phone. Why he asked me to call the radio station I don't know.

He asked me to write down the phone number and call them, to get through as he was coming home and would take over the call when he got there. I argued a bit against him, I didn't want to do it, but he pushed so much I relented. What did it matter? I wrote down the number as he told me and then hung up, started calling the radio station for him.

Either he gave me the wrong number to call, or I wrote it down incorrectly but either way when I called the number, it was not a recognised telephone number. I froze, scared of having to tell him that I wasn't able to get through. Whatever the competition was, he felt entitled to win it, it was important to him. As such, I was already at this stage, scared of telling him I wasn't able to complete the task he had given me.

That is what caused him to physically become violent towards me that afternoon. I calmly told him I wasn't able to get through. He accused me of deliberately sabotaging him, that because I had not wanted to do it, I had not bothered to write down the number properly or listened to him. Honestly, I did, I paid attention, and this was either just a genuine mistake on my part or a mistake he made in giving me the wrong number.

He exploded, I ran through to the kitchen, and he caught up to me. He grabbed me by the throat and pinned me to the cupboard door, hard. I was scared. I had never seen him so angry. He was screaming at me. Like I said above, it all happened very quickly and was over just as fast.

I had no idea what to do so I continued my day as best I could.

***

One time he did show his true colours in front of another person was a midwife at around 40 weeks pregnant in an appointment for a sweep. If you don't know what a sweep is, it's where a midwife sticks their finger inside your vagina and literally "sweeps" the area to help trigger birth.

He accused me of cheating by having this done.

It was a mandatory appointment in the progression of being pregnant. Like the Anti-D injections, I had to get, because I'm rhesus negative my blood type is 0 negative, or ultrasounds.

The midwife sat us both down afterwards to have a chat about my body and how I was feeling etc offering to answer any questions we may have about the upcoming birth of our first child. He flipped out when she booked me in to be induced and it happened to be on a day that was inconvenient to him.

He argued with her about changing the day for me to be induced. She rightly argued back, telling him that there's a fine line of dates with inducing because if it goes on any longer then there is a risk to the baby, and me. The baby can die.

Still, he argued with her to the extent that he got up and stormed out.

She looked at me with pity, I looked at her with shame and embarrassment. She quietly told me that I didn't have to put up with his behaviour and she's perhaps the only one who ever said this to me. I apologised to her for his behaviour, told her that he was stressed about his job and the birth of our child. There was a lot of pressure on him.

She looked at me again with pity, tried to reassure me but I was already gaslighting myself and everyone else that he was a good man. Trying to prove I was loyal; to help and protect him, my husband.

I learned far too late that protecting someone, isn't being loyal, it isn't even being kind. It's the opposite. It just enables abusive behaviour to continue.

What I also never gave myself credit for at the time was how strong I was, I never even realised. My life was starting to fall apart; the cracks were visible. I stood tall and no matter how difficult things were or became, I did my best to keep moving forward and never gave up. I was under the same pressures he was, and I outperformed him every time.

Giving birth

I was terrified on the day I was induced; I had been for weeks leading up to it. Allan was not supportive during the birth and quickly started playing the victim. He complained how hard it was for him not being able to get food or that I didn't want him sitting on his phone speaking to every person he knew instead of me.

He kept trying to escape because he was bored. I just wanted him there with me, I was scared, and I was in pain. My anxiety kept telling me that the baby would be born still, and I was terrified. I needed his support, my hand to be held. He kept calling people, texting people and talking to everyone except me. He was also on the phone in front of me, complaining about me to everyone he spoke to. I know it must be hard to sit there for such a long time, but the selfishness wasn't lost on me.

I was lucky during the 15 hours and 17 minutes from when I was induced to giving birth without surgery that I only had a small vaginal tear. No one really prepares you for what happens during birth, the actual pain, the effects of the drugs administered and what happens to your body throughout the whole event. It was horrible and not something I wished to have happen ever again. I was an only child myself and I had always wanted one child, that was enough for me. Still, my vagina was mostly intact, and I was grateful for that. There were a lot of complications around my daughter's birth, she could have died but nothing I am willing to share. All I'll say is that again, he was as unsupportive as you can imagine.

***

I have been raped thousands of times. Not once, not twice... Not ten times or twenty times, not a hundred... I have been raped thousands of times.

The first time he raped me was within the two weeks of having my daughter, my first child, our first child (supposedly, his first child. That's a can of worms for later).

After the birth there was a male doctor who did a physical internal exam on me, while Allan was in the room, I add. I do have to add because again, he accused me of cheating on him, by allowing this male doctor to put his fingers inside of my vagina to examine me.

That was literally this man's job.

This was within the first day of giving birth because we were discharged quickly. It was a horrible and traumatic experience for both me and my daughter, and it could have been a lot worse. Despite not being allowed to act like that because it's just giving birth.

I was lucky I only had a small vaginal tear. Not bad considering she was 8.5lbs. The doctor gave me the option of having stitches, I had a strange aversion to getting stitches down there and asked if it was necessary. He agreed that although they would be dissolvable, due to my concerns about it, he wouldn't force me to get it done. We agreed to no stitches, but he made a point of saying to Allan specifically that there should be no sexual intercourse for a minimum of two weeks due to risk of not only infection but also tearing further and causing more complications.

This seemed extremely reasonable to me and since I was bleeding huge amounts of blood for days afterwards, exhausted from lack of sleep and honestly felt like I had been hit downstairs by a fucking sledgehammer. Sex was the last thing on my mind. What I wanted was sleep and rest and more sleep.

One night in bed however Allan rolled over on top of me where I had been lying on my back trying to sleep. He told me he was having sex with me. I reminded him what the doctor had told us, and he said he didn't care, that there was no way he could last as long as two weeks. How unfair that was and how I was his wife, how he had the right to do whatever he wanted to me.

He hurt me that night. Not physically like hitting or kicking me. He hurt my vagina when he penetrated me dry. It hurt badly; I was scared he had torn me like the doctor had warned. He raped me.

I was so confused by what he had done and the fact that he had done it at all. I had stayed quiet, crying a little in pain and he told me to "shh" and that it would be over soon.

Like yeah, I know but that's neither a good thing for me nor a compliment to you so…

I was so sleep deprived that I couldn't, didn't react as how I would have wanted. He surprised me so much by putting his full weight on top of me. I had no fight, no energy to push him off me.

When he was done, he just rolled off me again, turned away from me and went to sleep.

Just like that, he was out like a light and had probably had a great night sleep. He slept through our child waking up to be fed while I sat in bed crying, holding my baby and watching Buffy the Vampire Slayer. I was so tired, so bone weary and exhausted and I had no idea what to do.

I had never felt trapped like this.

I could only cry as I lay her down to sleep and had nothing else to do but try and sleep myself.

Adjusting to a new baby

I have never slept well but I've never known sleep deprivation and exhaustion the way of having an abusive husband combined with having a newborn baby.

He never once got up during the night to feed not only his daughter, but his son when he later came along. He did, however, tell anyone who would listen to him that he was the one doing the nightly feeds. Suggesting that I was too lazy and selfish to get up. He went out of his way to paint me as a bad mother right from those very first days. I rarely had the energy to defend myself.

It was a running joke that he had bought a sofa bed from Ikea for our daughter's bedroom. He did this so that I could sleep in the spare room with the baby on nights that he had to get up early for work, so that his sleep wasn't disturbed.

One day early on in her life, I was so tired that I was struggling to bathe her, he offered to take over. I was overwhelmed by him taking an interest in his child and offering to help me. I was overjoyed. That, like everything else with him was over quickly as within seconds, he screamed for me to come through. I had already set up the baby bath on the floor in her bedroom, it had barely any water in it as instructed. He panicked, I'm not sure if it was genuine fear or an act. He asked me to take her, to bathe her myself. He did apologise stating, he was scared he would hurt her. I had no choice but to take over and struggled to ask for help or give him any responsibility again.

It was most likely weaponized incompetence. He knew that if he took long enough to perform a task, I would go ahead and do it myself. If he chose not to bathe the kids, I would do it because it needed to be done. If I asked him to put clothes into the washing machine, he knew if he left it long enough, I would go and do it myself. It wasn't fair and I carried the household labour and all physical tasks of looking after the kids by myself. Unintentionally, he trained me to be a single mother.

He would also pretend to fall asleep a lot or just go to bed and fall asleep before I had a chance to ask anything or say something. I would try and wake him up; he just refused to wake up.

In those first few weeks, he would come home and immediately start screaming at me for the house being messy. "What have you been doing all day?" Those kinds of statements and questions. Sometimes this made me burst into tears at the shame and exhaustion I was feeling. Other times I would be so numb I couldn't take on how abusive he was being towards me.

He would then move onto screaming at me for not being presentable. I had once been well put together, yet at this time, it was easier not to wear makeup. Most days I hadn't even been able to bathe or eat because I couldn't physically put her down. She was the type of baby that screamed every single time she was put down in her crib, playpen, cot etc.

It didn't matter. No one's advice worked and trust me when I say, I absolutely asked everyone for tricks and nothing worked. I read books, I watched things on TV, nothing worked. The only thing that helped was as she became bigger, and able to move about a little more, I was able to take her with me and include her in whatever I was doing.

He would as a result make me feel a million times worse about myself as I knew I probably smelled like baby vomit and hadn't brushed my hair. I was still in my pjs most days. I'd ask him to look after her while I took a bath, we didn't even have a working shower in that rental house. He'd say no, that he had friends coming round or that he was going out with friends and it would have to wait until he got back.

That just made me remember how he would invite friends round constantly without telling me they were coming over.

He told me to go and see his gran if I was feeling overwhelmed. I felt uncomfortable going to his gran for help, not knowing why and he gave me shit for it. How nice they are, celebrated foster carers after all. He made me feel like I was a bad person for not acting more like family towards them. I just had a feeling not to, as it turned out, I was right to feel like they were unsafe, because they were. I didn't know it at the time.

I was on maternity leave from work and ended up going back to university two weeks after she was born.

Trapped.

Something inside of me rejected the rental house we were in, maybe it was being assaulted in my bedroom and kitchen that made me feel traumatised every time I was in the house. Perhaps it was the trapped feeling I had of being forced to stay home as he went off to work and spent time out with friends and family. His plan for us had been to buy a house and at the time, I didn't care, I just wanted out of that house. A new house, a home for us with our new baby would be perfect. A fresh start.

We found a house we liked, did all the applications, submitted all our ID, payslips, bank statements etc and were rejected. It turned out I was not accepted because of poor credit. After getting a look at my credit report it turned out I was hugely in debt. My mother had used my name and date of birth, her address to take out multiple catalogues and ran up around £10,000 that she had stopped paying back. I didn't even know about these catalogues, or of these accounts. This was done without my knowledge or consent. You might think, surely not your own mother? This was the first but not the last time she did this.

Allan was furious, he was so angry that we lost that house and I was therefore unable to be put on a mortgage and his plans were ruined as a result. He wanted to speak to my mum; I begged him not to. He wanted to go to the police; I begged him not to. As much as I was furious with her, it felt like something she would do. This was a woman who had abandoned her pregnant daughter, never reached out to me or did anything unless Allan forced her to, or I had to be the one to constantly fix these bridges that she kept burning. Either way I felt bad about it and didn't want to cause any trouble. I was also embarrassed by it. This was another thing he was angry about towards me, as he took out a loan to clear off all the debt in my name so that I had none in the hope of me being accepted for a second mortgage application.

We learned quickly that's not how that works. Instead, he convinced his father to become guarantor on the mortgage which was solely in Allan's name. He would continue to throw this in my face to remind me it was, "his house." This was even despite the lawyer at the time telling us that no matter if it was solely in his name, that because we were married the house was just as much mine. That never sat right with him. He had convinced his father he would only be guarantor for a short time, as we would wait for my credit to go back to normal and remortgage, taking his name off and putting mine on instead.

This was October/November 2007, and it was right before the housing market crashed. We possibly got one of the last 100% mortgages in the country. We didn't pay a deposit and overpaid wildly on the house itself. It was afterwards only valued at 80k when we had offered and had a mortgage for 95k. This made things extremely difficult financially for us going forward. It was another trap and reason it became difficult to leave later.

***

Physically he started off by using his size against me. I was always so much smaller than him in height and weight. He used his body to block my way, to stop me from leaving rooms when I was trying to remove myself from the situation. He learned very quickly that I was a reactive person, always blowing up with little emotional regulation. He did this deliberately by bullying me, teasing me and ultimately from watching and getting to know all my triggers. This was intentional and intent is where abusive manipulation comes from. Anything can be a red or green flag, the real concern is what is the person's intent behind what they have said or done.

He knew I didn't like small spaces, he knew I didn't like being cornered so he would intentionally use his height, weight and broadness to trap me in spaces and then laugh at me, asking me what was I going to do about it?

This would cause me to panic, he would induce panic attacks in me and then get off on watching me react physically. I would shove him to get past him. The moment I put my hands on him; to push him away from me or anything like that, it was a green light to attack me physically. He used this reasoning to rationalise the fact that he was then, "protecting himself from me."

That felt like a complicated thing to try and explain to anyone. It also tripped me up in court much later because it was hard to explain.

Now, it's extremely important to say that I verbally communicated clearly to him how I felt in the moment about this. And soon, realising what game he was playing and what he wanted from it, I had to make sure I was clearly, enunciating and communicating that I felt trapped & I felt scared. If he did not back off, if he did not give me space, then I would use any force necessary to free myself.

I spoke clearly before and after even though I was having a panic attack, but I still had to teach myself to communicate because he afterwards blamed me solely for attacking him and pitched it to me that it was completely unprovoked on my part.

This infuriated me because not only would he do this in front of the kids who were little more than babies and toddlers at this point, I also knew he was wrong. I felt in danger and couldn't understand why he was doing this. My incessant need to always understand people and situations is one of the worst things about me that had constantly and consistently ended me up in nothing but trouble.

He was always lying, blatantly and to my face which I couldn't understand. Then he would give me what I felt was a logical answer. I would then start to question myself. Was I remembering it incorrectly? Was I more mentally ill than I realised? Was I hallucinating?

He used my fears over my mental health, my sleep deprivation, my own senses and memory against me.

He would also take time in between these incidents so that I would forget that they had even happened. This would also help me gaslight myself as I would honestly question, did I make it up? He hadn't done it again. In the early days, months could pass without an physically or sexually violent incident (he was emotionally abusive the whole time, sexually coercive and manipulative but I didn't understand those things at the time to know what was being done to me) and every day afterwards where he acted decent enough, as such, I started to believe I had made it all up.

Consent, I did not understand consent. I see so many people questioning if it was rape, did the other person know what they were doing? Here's how to reframe that properly; they are aware of what they are doing. They know and understand what consent is. That's why they go to such great lengths to confuse you, manipulate you through emotion, fake tears and gaslighting. That's intentional.

They are hoping that you don't understand consent.

If they confuse you enough, you will not be confident telling someone else.

That lack of confidence in what you're accusing makes you harder to believe.

He would tell me it hurt his feelings that I felt he could hurt me. How could I believe he would ever do such a thing to me? I once remember saying, "you hit me," and he started crying. Telling me in between sobs that he was so hurt that I could even think such a thing of him. How mentally ill was I, to accuse him of such a thing?

He used everything I was against me; my fears of my mental health, my lack of sleep from looking after two children and him, being the only one who did any housework, working and trying to keep him entertained. He said it was my fault, that I believed he was just like my father and that was unfair to him. That he would never hurt me.

I would become confused. I had been confident to begin with that I was right and yet, his confidence and his emotional reaction made me believe I might be wrong. What if I was?

I wish I had been.

THE TOWN-HOUSE

NOVEMBER 2007 – NOVEMBER 2017

Pushed too much too quickly

When I had gone on maternity leave, I had the intention of never going back to that job. I hated it, hated the atmosphere and again, just had a bad feeling about the whole place. We had spoken early on that I would concentrate at university and be a mum to our child. That he would be the one working, maybe I could get a part time job if I wished.

However, buying the house meant on paper having two incomes coming in and as such he forced me to go back to work 12 weeks after our daughter was born. Allan wanted more money. His job at the time paid less than mine did. Being on maternity leave and new at the job meant I was only getting statutory maternity pay, not the full salary he had liked me earning being at work. So, back to work I went, and it was done kicking and screaming because I was not ready.

The townhouse was everything I had wanted since I was a child. Frequently I had seen the glorious ex-council houses, the three level, four-bedroom, one bathroom & one separate WC, homes walking past and I had wanted one. It was at the time, my ideal home. I'd always dreamed of having a drum kit set up in the garage for me to play.

This one became ours in early November 2007. The current occupants asked for an extra week to move out and being kind, naive and youthful people, we agreed. A week later we moved. I had been back at work for a while; I went home to the new house and stayed up all night unpacking. Went to work again the next morning.

Quickly we learned that the shower was not working. When it was switched on it flooded the hallway underneath. There were loads of issues with the house, but we were out with the dates for complaining about anything, having given the old occupants time to move out. I loved that house though. Over time, it became unbearable to live in. Too many ghosts, too many horrible memories haunting me.

First Christmas with daughter and in the new house

He continued to be physically violent towards me but not yet punching me. He was extremely rough, would grab me & push me. He had slapped me at this stage before. Allan would try to block my way in and out of rooms. This was always deliberately trying to start arguments and push me into blowing up so he could tackle me and pin me to the floor.

I remember one Christmas he started screaming at me because we were late going to his parents and I was preoccupied with a surprise gift from my mum that I liked. His dad was even the one who had helped me set up the multiple CD player hi-fi that I had told my mum I liked but never expected her to get for me. Perhaps it was a gift to shut me up after what had happened earlier in the year.

Allan had become preoccupied with the fact that his mother was expecting us. That we had to leave. We were relying on his father to chauffeur us around as neither of us drove. It was his father who told him to stop shouting at me, that his mother could wait. I was only excited about my new gift after all.

He had wanted us to spend Christmas at his gran's, or his parents' house every single year. That we would always go to theirs for Christmas dinner. After carting around a baby that was only four months old, I told him categorically that I would never go to anyone's house ever again after that Christmas. Especially since he was pressuring me to have another baby at this time. The thought of two babies, no car of our own and bottles, changing bags etc while going from house to house to see everyone felt overwhelming. It wasn't the happiest Christmas that I could imagine. Especially since at his mother's I would be expected to be dressed up and presentable when Christmas to me is a new set of comfy PJs, not a dress and makeup.

It wasn't an ultimatum; it was a fact stated clearly and articulately. I was not prepared, especially with the likelihood of a second baby, to do Christmas anywhere except our own home. Christmas to me, was never about either of our blood families. It was now about my children, family could come to us and visit if they wanted to, they would be more than welcome. I wanted my children to be in their home, with their toys on their day and fuck anyone who didn't like that, including him.

I never said I was popular with anyone.

He called me a bitch and he wasn't wrong.

I did however end up taking over the mantle of Christmas dinner, at one point making it for twenty people. Multiple courses, multiple choices within the courses to accommodate everyone's food sensitivities, allergies and preferences. I did this because I cared about those people and wanted them to have a nice meal.

***

One week later, it was New Years Eve, and I was staring at a glass of champagne in my hand. The first champagne I'd had since I was raped in that club with him on a night out two Christmases past now. I stared at the glass, that one sip I had brought back the terror I felt that night with clarity I didn't like. I also knew without a doubt that I was pregnant again. I never drank alcohol during either pregnancy. I'd barely stand close to anyone smoking cigarettes when pregnant. I was extremely careful.

I was scared and I felt trapped.

New year, new him?

It took a few weeks for the tests to show as positive. I remember being at work, it was a Wednesday, and I went to the manager there and told them I was sick. I needed to go home. I don't get sick, I'd only ever vomit with alcohol or an extreme sickness bug, so I knew I needed to get home. I couldn't stay at work. The manager panicked, seeing my distress and offered to drive me to the doctors.

As we got there, we found the surgery closed because of course, I had forgotten at the time they closed on Wednesday afternoons for staff training. Craig offered to drive me home. Shortly afterwards I walked to the shop, bought some pregnancy tests and took them home. That was when I got the positive result.

Despite going out of his way to get me pregnant, he accused me of his son, not being his. Every single man at my work was a suspect, every person I had ever spoken to or had been around was a suspect. Everyone from his own brother and father to all his friends. It was exhausting. He had wanted me pregnant and now I was pregnant. I should have had my feet up, relaxing and I was being verbally assaulted and mentally tortured by these constant accusations.

It wasn't just him snapping at me that I had "fucked so-and-so," it was the games he would play to try and get me to confess to cheating on him. Telling me that a friend of his had told him in confidence that we'd cheated behind Allan's back. I would have to defend myself constantly. This was a daily occurrence.

Or he would sit me down and say he found something on my phone, that he had "seen the texts." It was all a manipulation tactic to get me, if I had felt guilt over cheating, would overshare and tell him. He had never seen any texts on my phone because there were never any texts like that on my phone. I wasn't allowed a password on my phone. He took my phone from me constantly. He would read all my messages and even reply to people, pretending to be me.

I may have emotionally cheated, needing connection with another human being who wasn't him but aside from one night in 2010, which I still to this day have no idea what happened, I never physically cheated on him. That night as far as I am aware, could have been another game he was playing. Maybe something worse happened, I don't know. I only know what he told me, and then what the police later told me.

Both of his children however were his without a doubt.

At this stage, I was too fucking tired to even pretend to be nice to other people. I wanted to be left alone. I used to make jokes about wanting to go on holiday by myself. To get a hotel room somewhere with the intention of genuinely sleeping for the entire time, by myself. Not speak to anyone, not interact with anyone. Literally, sleep in a bed without him harassing me.

Such a charmer

Valentine's Day and my first one at this job which I started in March the previous year. I was excited and it was lovely to see massive bunches of flowers being delivered to some of the women in the office. It was an odd place because the main centre manager and one of the other important people in charge were both women, both in relationships and both received massive bunches in beautiful shades of colours. It was a small office where everyone knew each other well and there were cheers for everyone when these flowers came at different intervals during the day.

I was shocked when an equally large bunch arrived in the late morning and were given to me. I was pregnant and felt unimportant, so being the centre of attention at that point was lovely. I was one of the group and not the outsider that I always felt like.

It wasn't the worst place I had ever worked but it was toxic; the pay was scarily good for what we did, it was at the time, easy work. They had a recruitment recently and interviews scheduled for that day. Most of the people being interviewed were friends or family of those who already worked there, there was an incentive scheme to refer people which also paid well. As I was good at writing, I had done Allan's CV and application for him.

He had been working in a job he liked that made him feel good about himself, but the pay was rubbish, and his contract was zero hours. Although he always got a solid 40 hours every week, his paranoia especially with a mortgage, baby and another baby on the way meant he was constantly stressed about that possibility where he may get less than the 40 hours.

So, he had applied at my workplace and his interview was today. He was being interviewed by my manager, Amy, who adored me, and I was one of few women that she seemed to get along with. She cared a lot about me, I could tell, she was always rather protective and was beaming when I received my flowers, knowing that Allan was due in later that afternoon.

When he arrived, Amy went to introduce herself to him and he was given a little tour. The workplace being what it was, they made a big fuss over him going on about what an amazing husband he was to have been so thoughtful to send his pregnant wife such a beautiful bunch of flowers. They couldn't get over how well he had chosen the flowers and how lucky I was to have such a partner.

Unsurprisingly his interview went extremely well. He was hired and started working there a few weeks later. He was always amazing at talking to people, charming and so unassuming in looks that he was easy to believe and came across very likeable. At least at face level and until anyone got to see too much of him. Little ugly parts of his personality would leak out; he was good at fooling people you see but even he didn't completely understand people.

Sometimes he got things wrong and showed a little too much of his real self, it was only ever really a glimpse, but it was enough that some people avoided him, probably without realising they were in the presence of such a prolific predator.

I will be vain and fickle here, but I loved getting flowers delivered at work on Valentines Day. I absolutely loved it. It was great getting that little bit of attention, showing everyone how loved and lucky I was, even if it was a lie. Maybe especially because it was a lie. For many years I felt entitled to gifts as if he couldn't show me real love then surely at least he could buy me pretty things to ease my suffering? After a while that stopped working but I never forgot about those flowers.

I expected them every year after that, thinking that if he bought me them on his previous salary then he could afford them every year thereafter as he was on double, probably closer to triple the pay.

Never again did I have a bunch of flowers delivered to me from him. Never to work and never to home. I did occasionally get a bunch bought at the shop and brought home to me. Mostly I assumed as an apology for something he had done to me, that he wanted forgiveness for but did not deserve it. Thinking that flashing something shiny would make me forget whatever it was he had done.

It took me until after he was arrested to realise that those flowers were never meant for me as a thoughtful, caring gesture. He had used me to manipulate the people conducting his interview, to buy their affection to get the job. They weren't for me at all; they were an investment for his future.

First holiday together

We only went on one holiday together as a couple. It was in May 2009. It was a disaster, we argued constantly. I was realising that the only thing we had in common were the children.

He called me ungrateful because I didn't appreciate the house, the kids and the nice things he bought me. I didn't care about a single thing he did or could buy me. In the beginning there was a lot of money, I never saw it because he never let me have access to the bank account. Originally I had managed the month-to-month budget until he took over while I was pregnant with our son. He did this to help ease my burdens, but I never had free access to the bank account to buy myself or anyone else anything. I wasn't allowed to spend the money, I had to ask his permission before doing so. Most of the time he would say no.

He did buy me a lot of nice, shiny, expensive things. Mostly things I hadn't asked for. He'd buy me jewellery that was the wrong colour, clothes that he liked, not clothes that I wanted.

I was called ungrateful and selfish. I didn't care about the material things, what I wanted was not to be hit, not to be raped. I wanted peace and quiet; a safe home. He felt if he spent money on me, then I should just shut up about it and let him do whatever he wanted to me.

"You cheated on me! Of course you did!" He screamed at me, unhinged and believing his nonsense completely. I had just gone for a walk on the beach because I was angry at his constant bullying. Were people able to meet someone so quickly and have sex? Had I been gone longer than half an hour? Does he not realise how anxious I am that I don't talk to people I don't know? I hate seeking comfort in others and dislike small talk even more. Not to mention that I despise people touching me…

Did he honestly believe that was possible? Wait… Does that mean he has done that? Is that why he's accusing me, knowing that he can do these things therefore so must I?

***

Allan at one point said he wanted a football team worth of children. He wanted at least 10. I told him to fuck off. Of course, he wanted that many kids, he didn't have to be pregnant. He didn't have to look after them. I said during my pregnancy with my son that I would not have another, that no matter what happened with this pregnancy, it would be my last.

Eventually he agreed, seeing in real time how expensive having kids was and how inconvenient they were for him. The reality hit him hard. I had gone to the GP and at the age of 23, they practically laughed me out of the Doctor's office. The idea being that I was too young to understand what I wanted, that I might change my mind. I got asked a million questions around Allan and what he wanted. I was asked, "what if one of your children dies..." I've never understood the idea of replacing children personally.

I pushed, I was fed up and scared of falling pregnant. Birth control has never been reliable for me. I was terrified. I eventually got put on the waiting list to be sterilised.

However, Allan decided he would take one for the team and get a vasectomy. Now, I probably joked about him getting one done but it's important to know that I wanted to be sterilised. I wanted to make sure that I could never get pregnant again. I had major anxiety over this. I sit here now, wishing I had gone ahead and gotten it done at the time. I am again back on the NHS waiting list to get it done now. He volunteered to get the vasectomy, saying that he didn't want me to go through such an invasive operation or deal with the recovery.

I don't feel he did this for my benefit. Nor am I convinced it was done at all.

My mental health got WORSE

I never had any anxieties or concerns about my son as a baby; I took to motherhood in a way I hadn't with my daughter. Having confidence made me a more relaxed, logical, ultimately a better parent. It wasn't until Allan had sat me down one evening after I had done the kids' bedtime routine all by myself as usual, with a movie that my brain broke.

It was a horror, he had been excited to watch it, and horror had always been something we had bonded over. Poor boy, always telling himself he did things with the best intentions and yet this was the one decision he made that fucked things up colossally for us both.

The movie opened in black and white and focused on a couple who were passionately having sex. I was now at the point of being embarrassed watching anything sexual with him. He made me uncomfortable, and I knew it would turn him on, that he would be expecting things to happen either during or afterwards. I would have to go along with it or risk being hurt again.

The movie was beautiful, black and white with no talking if I remember correctly, I believe there was music playing but I honestly can't remember now. It was switching from scenes of them being passionate with one another to scenes of their baby boy in his crib. The child was awake. The child was adorable; blue eyed and blonde hair and was younger than our son but they looked so much alike.

I couldn't help but criticise the choices the parents had made with the child. The crib was still in the newborn position of having the base raised. The child was too big for that; I remember saying to Allan that he's going to climb out and he did. It was clear from the scenes going back and forth that the parents were too wound up with one another that they were not paying attention to the baby monitor or anything else and were completely unaware of what was happening.

The child leaves the bedroom and walks down the hall. Again, I remember complaining about this too, they had a massive window left open in the hall. It was snowing and the child moved towards the window, its little legs wobbling along as it made its slow way towards the snow, hands outstretched and of course what happens? The child falls out of the window and dies. The parents not realising until sometime later. I had to stop watching the movie, I've never seen the rest. The movie is called Antichrist, and it came out on DVD to rent, here in the UK in January 2010.

I am hyper aware of my surroundings, and I live my life as a constant risk assessment. I simply notice things more than other people, but it's always confused me as to why other people don't see the risk in things the way I do. That one scene, that one realisation of not being aware enough of every situation that I may not have control over everything every single moment of the day, was scary. That I could be distracted and something bad might happen to one or both children. That changed me to my core that day.

I stopped consenting to sex with Allan that very moment. Never again did I consent. My anxiety told me that if I had sex with him, I wasn't paying attention to the kids, and they would die. If I took my eye off them for a second that they would die, and it would be my fault.

He never understood. He only became angry and grew angrier over the years. It never changed. I truly believed the kids would die if I distracted myself at all with anything or anyone.

I know what this is and it's something I've never been formally diagnosed with. Telling my husband who had already been pushing my boundaries, ignoring my consent and using coercion that I refused to ever have sex with him again was never going to go well. He refused, absolutely decided at that moment that his best course of action was to completely ignore my wants and needs and take whatever he wanted, whenever he wanted.

This massively damaged my already fragile mental health and state of mind. I didn't have a choice in this. This was a compulsion.

Some reading this might think that this decision of mine was "unfair" on him but realistically I wasn't asking him to stay married to me and never have sex again. I told him he could leave. I knew my marriage was sinking, the abuse was unforgivable at this stage, and it only got worse with every year that passed. I told him to leave, to go and meet someone else who wanted to have sex. Someone fun, someone mentally healthy who wanted to be with him, someone who made him happy. He refused. He refused to divorce me, refused to let me leave or leave himself.

Since that film came out in 2010, I know that every sexual experience I had with him from this moment onwards was rape; coerced or violent, it was never consensual again. All the earlier times? I don't remember clearly enough and wasn't educated enough about coercion, manipulation, gaslighting, guilt tripping etc. I know he was always raping me, but this is the one date I have I can get clear in my own mind.

The worst thing he had said to me... Up to that point

Some things people say stick with you forever; this conversation was one of them. I hated Allan for what he said to me and for me, this was the catalyst to much worse things than an insult from someone who was supposed to love me.

We were walking from the town centre to the local soft play area. I was pushing my son in his stroller while his sister bounced around beside me, wandering away, running around us both but never going far. He turned around to me as we were walking through the underpass and just said, for me at least out of nowhere, "You are fat and ugly. I don't want to have sex with you anymore. I want to start having sex with other people."

That sentence, or phrase has been forever branded into my brain. I cannot forget the words, but I will be honest and say I can't quite remember exactly what he said afterwards. I was quiet, he had achieved what anyone would have said was impossible and he shocked me into complete silence. My mouth hanging open in surprise, I didn't say anything. I was thinking though, and two things came to mind in that moment although I didn't think at that moment, I said them, I'm sure I did later though.

Who the fuck are you to call me fat and ugly?

You want to fuck other people? You mean you want to fuck Leslie…

I was insecure at that time. I was overweight in comparison to what people had known about me. I was still carrying all that weight I had accumulated while pregnant with son and having two small children and a complete fucking idiot for a husband kept me fat and eating badly. It was hard to have any time for myself where I could either prepare a decent meal or exercise. I didn't have free time anymore.

Leslie was new at our work and although her boyfriend Peter also worked in the same office, we all did, it was clear that Leslie liked Allan, and he liked her. It was awkward and he had embarrassed me many times by how often he spoke to her and the way he did. She was brazen and it pissed me off, but I had bitten my tongue. Not bringing it up to her at all and I never acted like it bothered me, it did though. She was a slightly younger but skinnier version of me. Even I could see the resemblance. She was younger, with no kids and much more fun than the sensible mother I had to be, mothering not only my own two children but my husband too.

She was normally blonde but had dyed her hair recently. A few days later Allan had come home from work and asked me to dye my hair red… I wasn't stupid, and all I could do was refuse.

I was insecure about myself and about her, but it still shocked me that he could be so horrible. It was insulting, not to mention that even though I was fat I was still beautiful. All his friends would have swooped me up in a heartbeat if they had the chance, I was wanted by everyone we knew, it was a constant source of arguments between us. The way his friends all spoke about me was filthy & disgusting. At the time I still thought this meant they liked me but they only viewed me as an object. Of course, now I know that's because pretty & dumb is what most men look for in a woman. I was that in abundance.

It wasn't until years later I realised that Allan wasn't annoyed at me for being "fat" or overweight. He was annoyed that my body had developed and changed, and I no longer resembled a child. I had the body of a woman now, with massive breasts, hips and a round ass. Things I had never had previously. Because the truth was, years later when I gained weight due to depression, he never cared about my weight at all. In fact, in those last couple of years together, he would actively tell me I was beautiful no matter my weight and I weighed more than I did at this time.

Alas, I was only twenty-four and sleep deprived, I lost my fucking mind over this and agreed to seek revenge, hit him where it really hurt. I devised a plan to flirt with all his friends in front of him the next time we were all together. I was going to show him that his fat and ugly wife was in fact, wanted by all his friends. That if I was to choose to, I could leave him for any of his friends, just like he had always been afraid of.

My mind was dangerously split between knowing he was abusing me and me still believing I was able to make my own choices. I wasn't able to choose anything for myself.

How fucking stupid could one person be? I was about to find out…

MAY 2010. His birthday.

The night of Saturday 8th May 2010 will haunt me forever. For this reason, I bring it up here, not because I want to tease the awful events of the night but because it deserves more time and space than I can give it in part one. I could probably write a book about this night alone. Mentioning it here is deliberate so that certain parties involved know that I haven't forgotten about May 8th 2010…

The first time he punched me in the face

The first time he punched me in the face truly took me by surprise. To me, in that moment it came out of nowhere but for him I see that he was just waiting to do it, no longer able to contain his genuine hatred for me. I hadn't done anything wrong. Not really. I'd tell him in later years that even if I had done all the bad things he had accused me of, I still did not deserve to be punched in the face. No one deserves that. The relationship should have ended so many times. I would hope to walk away from anyone now without a second thought, but it doesn't really work that way.

    I was at this point "nagging him" about something chore related, perhaps him not helping me with the laundry. On his phone, something he paid more attention to than he ever paid to me, he sighed before it happened. The next thing I know, he had thrown his fist out towards me and punched me square in the face. I fell backwards, clutching my face, believing he had broken my nose due to the pain. He hadn't. He exploded out of the chair he had been sitting in and flung himself towards me.

    I remember being so frightened by the violence and how much he had hurt me, that I turned my head to the left looking around desperately for something to protect myself with. I saw a heavy crystal candle holder his mother had gifted us. I picked it up, feeling the weight of it and in that moment, I went to hit him in the head with it. I didn't. Something in me stopped because even in that moment, that time when I was terrified and he was still hitting me, I knew it would kill him if I did. I put it down.

He continued hitting me, proceeding to rape me before eventually calming back down. He sat himself back in his chair with his phone and continued to ignore me as I just lay there on the floor not sure what had happened.

The smear campaign for me inevitably leaving him, started early

Standing in the middle of the town centre and letting him entertain his friend, I would have happily spoken to Sarah too. I liked her but the kids were bored and there was no sign of ever getting home. Too often Allan liked to have the kids out of the house for as long as possible. It was easier for him as he didn't have to worry about them interrupting his time spent on his phone or watching television.

    I sighed, having two children practically climbing over me wanting both mine and their father's attention. He was chatting away, and I was now used to blocking him out, his words practically went in one ear and out of the other. Sarah was moaning about her husband again, that's all she ever did but kept professing that she had loved him since she was thirteen years old, that she would always love him.

    She had told us many times that she cheated on him constantly with anyone that she could. That he had not wanted to get married despite them having a home and children together and that they only got married because she agreed to give him what he wanted, a threesome. It was with her best friend, and that friendship was difficult after that, they weren't ever really the same. Sarah was looking up at Allan, her lifelong bestie, with admiration as he was talking about how he did all the housework, that he regularly did the hoovering.

That got my attention, and I knew my facial expressions were a straight reflection of the thought that bounced about in my head.

Yeah, fucking right.

I bet he doesn't even know where I keep the hoover.

She was gazing at him almost lovingly, in an expression that made me feel sorry for her. What a fool she was to believe him. What trouble I was in though, that he could lie too easily to someone he told me that he cared about, loved dearly as a friend, even if it was something simple. It annoyed me because he did it for two reasons; one to make me look bad and two to make Sarah question her own relationship, knowing she could have better, that better was out there.

Shame she set her sights on him. I wasn't worried because he told me countless times when I had questioned his relationship with her that he wouldn't fuck her if she was the last person alive. That she was "dirty" and "used up" that he wasn't interested in someone who had been with so many partners.

I believed that. It seemed reasonable because he hated me badly for having had sex with someone before him. He wanted me to have been a virgin; he regularly told me how disgusted he was to think that someone else had their penis inside me before he did. I didn't have anything to say to that after all, how could I apologise for something that had happened before I had even met him? There was absolutely nothing I could do about it.

Another Valentine's and my hernia operation

Valentines Day 2011 was the scheduled day of my hernia operation. Allan had made the effort the evening before to make it special for me. For some reason unknown to me he liked to try on the holidays like this. Maybe it was so he could boast and tell other people. Maybe it was for the photo op on social media, to post pictures for others to gush about what an amazing husband he was.

Just weeks earlier he had also gotten the family a puppy. It was a half husky mixed with something I can't quite remember now, a gorgeous girl whom we named Popcorn. Just one of many funny named pets we would acquire and ultimately, I would rehome due to the neglect of the animal. I wanted the puppy, but I wasn't looking for a pet.

We had gone to the cinema on Monday night to see a comedy about an alien that I didn't enjoy. That was happening more often. I was finding it difficult to enjoy simple things like movies. Maybe I was a little worried about the operation too. It was to be a simple op, keyhole surgery but I wasn't worried about the operation itself, more the aftereffects of what he would be like while I tried to recover.

Using his horribly effective negotiation skills, he had managed to get rid of both kids, passing our daughter onto his mum & dad and son to my mum stating that he would be unable to look after the kids, that he would have to look after me. No one believed him but everyone humoured him and did as they were told. I often wondered if anyone realised they were being played, manipulated or if it was just too much hassle to argue against him. I knew the feeling.

So, on Tuesday I went to the hospital and awaited surgery. I had been born with a hernia, it had accompanied me throughout my life, and I had forgotten about it. Until I started getting pains following giving birth to our son and gotten worse in those few years. The lump was just above my belly button and protruded every time I ate or drank anything at all. It was worse with fizzy juice which I reluctantly had to give up at this point. The agony it would cause was unholy.

Then came my surgery and all went well, it was over quickly with zero complications. I was taken to recovery and woke up before I left the operating room. I did however fall back asleep quite quickly, overcome with exhaustion as the night before I hadn't slept. Both kids were sick with the cold, they barely slept which meant I had very little sleep. Despite being in a ward with other people, only a curtain separating me from others, I fell into a deep sleep that lasted a few hours.

I panicked when I woke up some time later, already dark outside and with over 20 missed calls on my mobile phone from Allan desperately seeking an update. He was out with our friend, and had arranged for Gerald to pick me up and take me home. A nurse came around to check on me and was concerned that I was so tired. I explained as best I could that I had two young children who were a handful and didn't like to sleep on a good night. I guess it was the first decent rest I had in years, being away from everyone like that, knowing the kids were safe as they were not with him. I had my stomach checked and she agreed that I could go home, if I went to the toilet and passed urine first. Then I would have to be picked up as soon as shortly they would not let me leave the hospital, would have to keep me in overnight.

As she left me, pulling the curtain back around me for privacy, I heard her laugh with her colleague when she went out of the ward. "You should the mess of that girl's stomach!" I may not be good at understanding subtext, metaphors or general social cues but it seemed clear even to me that whatever had been done to my stomach was unusual for that type of operation. "Great, that gives me loads of confidence," I thought to myself.

I looked at my stomach, blown up with the gas they had used to perform the operation, I'm assuming to give them more space to manoeuvre. It was shades of black, blue, yellow and red as I saw properly the seven incisions I had all over my stomach. There was one larger scar that ran from my bellybutton down to the top of where my pubic hair began. It was the biggest of all the scars, the rest being small cuts which were dotted around the area. I was in a lot of pain, but the worst part was the scratchy dryness of my throat. I drank the water that the nurse had provided and longed for a large chocolate milkshake from a certain fast-food restaurant.

When I eventually phoned him back, he told me that he and Gerald had been waiting to hear from me, but they hadn't eaten yet (this was almost 9pm) and were going to get some food for themselves. I panicked, not wanting to stay in the hospital overnight, scared to do so, feeling vulnerable and somehow only safe from other people when I was with Allan. I heard the desperation as I begged him to come get me now trying to explain that it was late and if they didn't come right now to get me, I'd have to stay overnight. I knew he wouldn't want that either. Regardless of how much he hated my company he also hated me being away from him.

Eventually he agreed and he said they would come to pick me up. I pushed myself out of bed and tried to make my way to the toilets, knowing I'd have to pee before I'd be allowed to leave. I never did ask why but getting to the toilet itself was a nightmare. I realised then that the location of the operation was around my core muscles which screamed at me in agony as I tried to even sit up or swing my legs around. Terrified of bursting my stitches, scared they would have to be redone if I did that. I still pushed on, forcing myself knowing that Allan would be angry with me if I wasn't ready to be collected as soon as they arrived.

I panicked more when I eventually made it to the toilet and realised that I was completely unable to pee. I needed to, I had drunk a lot of water and hadn't been for more than half a day due to the operation and my unplanned nap. I was bursting and yet I could not make myself go. So, I did what I assume anyone would do in that position, I lied and told the nurse that I was able to pass urine. The look she had on her face was clearly unimpressed and unconvinced, but I pushed and pushed. She agreed I could go, giving me some painkillers and allowing me to leave with my husband who was clearly annoyed at having to come get me.

I was in pink fleece pyjama bottoms and a long-sleeved top which had hearts all over them. No jacket, and in my slippers as I walked through the hospital with him, thankful that he went slowly and wasn't charging off as he'd normally walk ahead from me. I had to use his arm to help me move. I was really struggling, the earlier painkillers clearly wearing off as I almost cried in pain as I walked the distance through the car park as he led me to Gerald's car. It felt like they had deliberately parked as far away as humanly possible.

I somehow managed to get into the back and they drove off, making their way to what would be open at the time, a fast-food restaurant. Maybe I'd be lucky enough to get my milkshake after all.

They parked and left me in the backseat as they went inside and ate. Allan eventually popped out with no food for me, but the large chocolate milkshake which was my go-to anytime I wasn't feeling well. He then returned to Gerald and sometime later they appeared. I was in agony, everything hurt, and my throat felt awful. I just wanted to go home to bed and sleep.

They all must hate me

Coming towards him, standing there next to someone's desk, talking away. I caught the end of a conversation, hearing my name and being interested about what they were talking about… "See, that's where you've got it wrong," he was saying. "If we're being honest..." He looked at me then, smiling as he spoke confidently and clearly, loud enough so that anyone in the immediate area could hear.

Since it was lunchtime and many people were eating at their desks, a lot of people would overhear. "It would be far more likely that Louise would hit me than I would ever hit Louise." The nods from the men he was standing with contributed to losing my appetite. That was how he was doing it. Little by little, conversation by conversation. Brazen, bold lies as he planted those seeds of doubt in others.

I see a lot of talk about smear campaigns after a breakup but mine started right at the beginning of the marriage.

If I ever spoke up, spoke out and told anyone, would they believe me? No… Judging from the nodding agreement and laughter from the men he was talking to. These were all men who I had known a few years of having worked here now, they were all agreeing with Allan that I was the one most likely to be violent. The implication being that if he did ever hit me, it would be in self-defence because I was the lunatic with the problem. Me? I was almost a foot smaller in height and weighed at my heaviest less than half his weight? Me? I was completely fucked.

***

A manager of ours, who was a friend of his once approached me and pulled me aside to ask, "Does Allan smoke weed?" I shook my head at Wilson, Allan was completely sober. He rarely drank, never showed any issues or left me wondering if he was taking drugs. "He's the most paranoid person I've ever known." He said and I shrugged at him, how was I supposed to respond? "Haha, yeah, he's a fucking lunatic, mate!" So I kept my mouth shut.

Allan was paranoid, he felt like everyone and everything was out to get him. He complained about people watching him, the police specifically. He would go on about hidden cameras, telephone conversations being recorded. So, he lied to everyone around him, manipulating situations and watching reactions trying to work out who was working against him. It was a chess game where he kept telling me that he liked being "at least ten steps ahead of everyone else." It sounded exhausting to me and I didn't take him seriously.

Now with some distance from him, I can see that he had every reason to be worried about the police investigating him.

A slip up

"Allan beats the shit out of me all the time."

Fuck!

The words were out of my mouth before I could even react. It was a one-to-one meeting with my boss at work. Normally I was on top of it all, juggling all his lies as best as I could. It went against me fundamentally as I'm usually brutally honest and unable to hold my tongue. It takes so much out of me to keep my mouth shut and this time it was a genuine accident. No, I had said it and I couldn't take it back! Or could I?

"Oh, I mean, like we hit each other of course, just regular little fights. Just like everyone has."

I saw the look on Dillian's face as it was serious in a way that he was rarely. Fuck. Fuck. Fuck. The little laugh I had thrown in at the end of that statement was hopeful enough to throw him off. I prayed anyway. Oh fuck! What would Allan do when it got back to him that I had told someone?

Over the years Allan tried to get promoted at this job. He had been in line for it, worked hard for it (Of course he made me do any written work for him). Was obsessed to the point that jokes were regularly made about how hard he tried and yet someone else was always picked instead of him. I was even offered a promotion over him, and had to turn it down because he was the one who wanted it.

I wondered if this one conversation I had with my manager at the time, got back to the main circle of the management team and this is the reason he was never selected. I don't think he ever knew about it. I'm confident he would have hurt me badly if he did, this promotion had meant so much to him.

I didn't deliberately sabotage him. It was a genuine slip-up based on constant frustration and fatigue, an exhaustion that comes from juggling too much. It was also a noose hanging just above my head. Something that weighed on me throughout the marriage as I waited for what he would do when he found out.

That was a new one

Sitting on the couch minding my own business I screamed out loud as he burst into the room, reaching me quicker than I had a chance to even realise what he was doing. Using his giant hands, he grabbed a handful of thick blonde hair and pulled me from the couch. I hit the floor with a thud as he dragged me by the hair across the living room laminate flooring and out of the open door. I cried at the pain, tried to struggle and get out of his grasp but he was too quick, not giving me a chance to do anything.

We reached the top of the stairs, and I did not think he would have been horrible enough to do what he did next. He kept proving me wrong. He went down the stairs and took me with him. He dragged me by the hair, his grip getting tighter as he went, taking me on my back, headfirst down the full flight of stairs. The harsh carpet scored my skin where it was bare, I was only wearing pjs, a vest and long fleece trousers, both in pink. I screamed and screamed.

At the bottom of the stairs before I had a chance to get my bearings or understand what was happening. Every part of me was sore from hitting the floor and stairs had banged my head repeatedly. He picked me up like I was nothing but a doll and opened the front door, throwing me out of it onto the pavement like I was trash.

It was cold out, still light but it was too cold for what I was wearing. I got up as quickly as I could, crying and in a lot of pain, all over my body. My head hurt. As I reached my hand up to feel my hair, I found clumps falling away in my fingers. I was scared and genuinely unsure of what had happened? Normally there was at least a reason for what he had done, what had happened? What had I done?

Outside our front door was not a garden. It was, like the other townhouses in the row, a pavement that ran along all the other houses. No one had a garden or even any partition between the houses and this was a shared car park for those who lived here. Across from that was a small grassy area and other houses which ran parallel from ours. I was mostly in the open as a result, I was conscious that anyone looking out of their window would have seen me standing there, messy hair and dishevelled pyjamas, no shoes or even socks on my feet and my face covered in fluids, from tears to snot to blood.

I moved towards the front door, finding it locked and began knocking on the door. As angry as I might have been at other times, I was too upset to be truly annoyed. I was scared. Scared because I didn't know if that was the end or just the beginning. I also felt responsible for keeping up appearances with both the neighbours and the kids. He acted like he cared for people's opinions yet in these moments he did very little to hide what he really was underneath the persona he had created. I knocked at the door and tried to keep myself composed because there was a chance that one of the kids would open the door and see me standing there, I didn't want to frighten them.

Trying to break my neck?

Another aspect of physical abuse that he started and used consistently because he quickly learned that it caused a surge of panic in me. This made me more compliant with his requests and was something he started before he turned to strangling me regularly. This was almost a build-up, a fascination with my neck that he seemed to have.

While he was physically attacking me, he would grab a hold of my face, his large hand covering a significant portion of my lower face, my mouth and nose usually (that's something else we will come back to) and push back. His strength was much greater than that of mine. He overwhelmed and overpowered me easily.

It was in moments like this I knew that no amount of me trying to hit him, of me scratching or kicking out at him would do anything. I was a mouse being dangled by the paw of a cat. There was no way I would ever win in a fight against him. That panic would be coarse through me in moments like this, being terrified of him snapping my neck.

The pain was unbearable and tied together with the fear of him breaking my neck, that felt like a very real possibility. Now, could he have broken my neck? With his size and strength, I think he held back a lot, he would say so. I'd complain about how hard he'd punch me, and he gave me this incredulous look and laughed a little, saying, "I never hit you full force" or "I could hit you harder."

He would be towering over me, encapsulating my space and allowing me no air or room to breathe as he pushed my head backwards as far as he could and kept trying to push back further. It felt now, looking back, like he was always experimenting with exactly how far he could take things.

The day before he was arrested, one of the last things he said to me after attacking me was how much he wished he could kill me, but everyone would know that he had done it. He was genuinely, or seemed that way at least, annoyed at not being able to do just that. How he would not escape the consequences of those actions and how put out that clearly made him feel.

He would push and push, I'd be crying, not able to scream or at least make any real noise because my mouth would be covered and I'd be scared I was going to die.

How many times, how many thousands of times did I sit or lie there in front of him, making peace with the fact that this was it. This was how it happened, and this was the last thing I would ever have any conscious awareness of. It wasn't rage I'd feel in those moments; it was utter defeat.

I think that is worse somehow. There's no poetry about it; no rising hero, no story of bravery. I was alone and I was scared, and I was utterly at the mercy of this man who claimed to love me.

I do not like, even now, discussing the physical things that he did to me because of the lasting, damaging psychological and physical effect that it had on me. I get a lot of neck and shoulder pain, I realised this will be residual from the sheer volume of trauma that was done to those parts of my body. My neck and shoulders are generally stiff and uncomfortable. But the psychological damage from having such things done, the fear that was intentionally inflicted towards me. How often I felt like I was about to die and then, having to get up and on with my day like it never happened.

In those moments the fear removes the ability to rationalise or intellectualise what a person is doing or why. Flight or fight, or in my case would always start with fight, freeze would eventually kick in when panic finally surfaced and I'd be trying to survive moment to moment. That's what living with domestic abuse is like, not surviving week by week but moment by moment. Every single second you are tense and aware of everything around you.

The last date I was on was about a year ago now, and as we were waiting for our coffee order in a busy cafe, said date was surprised that I was able to hear our names being called when he didn't. There was so much noise around us. And yet, I heard it immediately and without fail. This is due to hypervigilance, you live in a state of risk assessing everything in the surrounding areas. Watching for every moment so you can prepare what to do next. It's exhausting and again, five years after Allan's arrest, it was interesting to me that I was still living like that.

Of course, the autoimmune disorder from all the stress and being perpetually stuck in survival mode, is also a testament to that.

I realise now that Allan was experimenting with how much he could put me through physically and seeing how I reacted to it psychologically. He was trying to train me like a dog, make me more compliant, more submissive. Unfortunately for Allan he chose a difficult test subject to take (or maybe that's also exactly what he wanted, I'll never know) because he proved it himself that I cannot be trained by any amount of violence. I do not have a submissive bone in my body. No matter how often he beat me & raped me, no matter how seriously, how much pain he inflicted, it never mattered. Afterwards I would still give him the finger and call him a "rapist cunt" and stare at him out. I'd look down on him rather than putting him on any pedestal because I knew what he was.

I knew he was nothing but a sad, piece of shit who had all the options at his disposal to have made something of himself and instead chose not to. The simple fact about Allan is that the only good thing about him was me. I knew it, and he knew it and what pissed him off the most is that he knew that I knew it. I was simply better than him, it's not arrogance to say that it's the truth. I was smarter, I was prettier, I was nicer and generally more interesting than he was. He stole my whole personality, shaped himself after me because he studied me for years. He watched me and had become so enmeshed with me because of his co-dependency, that he could not function properly without me.

He did over time break down any self-assurance or confidence I had until I felt as bad about myself as he did about himself. It's taken a lot of hard work to get myself back to a place of loving each part of myself for who I am, as anyone deserves to.

I learned over time that I was his mirror, every bad thing he said about me is what he felt about himself. Every bad thing he accused me of, were things he had done himself. Every bad thing he did to me, he was doing to himself. Whether or not he has any mental health issues is not my place to say, I'm not a professional. My issue with him always was and will be that he never did anything to fix it.

I have mental health issues; it's obvious sitting down and having a conversation with me that there is "something not quite right with her." I know, I'm aware, I have been on the receiving end of bullying and fake concern for my whole life because of my mental health. I've also never shied away from topics like suicide, self-harm and how depression has affected me. People in general are always champions for mental health until they must hear about the genuine horrible and awful side effects and actual symptoms of said mental health disorders. Don't get me wrong, opinion overall is better and moving in the right direction but it's as if depression and anxiety are more generally understood and accepted but anything else is still demonised.

Back to my original point, is that he did this to me, pushed my neck to a literal breaking point to instil fear so that the next time he did such a thing (which ended up being daily) I would react better, do what I was told without him having to go through the full pantomime of kicking my ass into submission before being able to rape me. I think, sometimes he wanted to have the illusion that the rape was consensual sex. He cared nothing about me experiencing any pleasure but in some moments, he seemed to want it to be because I wanted it and not him having to force it.

I personally find that hard to believe because I can't imagine doing that to someone else. In any scenario, what turns me on is a mutual passion for one another. I've only kind of experienced that with one person but again, he turned out to just be mirroring my enthusiasm and didn't seem to care about me at all. I have only consensually had sex with three men in my lifetime. For all the times Allan has called me a slut and a whore (and I don't slut shame, although I do think that men should be called out for them being sluts because it is a negative attribute of the patriarchy and misogynistic for a man to be encouraged to be unfeeling towards their female partners and aim for numbers of conquests over genuine emotional connection.) it does make me laugh though that I really haven't had a lot of sexual partners or experiences. It's lonely being abused, I crave and fear the physical intimacy and sex that I feel I've missed out on, that I may never experience.

He hurt me to make me learn how to behave in a manner that he wanted me to act for him. Allan was devoid of realising that I had feelings and emotions independent from his own. I believe that he still has an image in his head of how I was at eighteen and never allowed me the grace to grow up and mature as I did. My body changed, my beliefs changed, my wants and desires changed, my ambitions changed.

He constantly stated how much I changed over the years and said it like it was a bad thing. You're supposed to change. Motherhood changes a person, being in school, college, university and then working jobs changes a person. Buying and running a household changes you. Children, marriage, friendships everything changes you, or at least it should. That is normal growth in life.

Allan however never changed, not once and not in any way that was real or tangible. He never grew up or matured, never changed his beliefs or attitude. He never changed his style or even his haircut since I first met him, the only thing that forced a change in that later in life was the balding and hair thinning that came on and got worse after I left. Those changes were forced upon him, out of his control. His weight progressively went up over the years as his lifestyle became more sedentary. For someone who only ever sat on his arse, he seemed to find new ways to ensure he sat on his arse for longer.

Accusing me? Of cheating? Don't make me laugh

"Neither of those kids are mine."

Again, again the same damn conversation kept coming up. I was getting bloody sick of it. "I don't believe what you said about Chris, that night he brought you home from work."

I was fucking fed up with it. I was tired, exhausted from lack of sleep and children who like to get up earlier every day it seemed. Both were hyper and prone to catching coughs and colds from other kids at school. Always sick and passing germs around the four of us in the house. I was running on empty now and pissed off at the constant accusations. I would understand if they were true but what annoyed me was that he never believed me. Never took my word or even listened to my side of things. He had his mind made up and nothing I said ever made a difference.

Chris was a guy I sat next to at work in the months leading up to me getting pregnant with my son, and before Allan started working there himself. He had offered one night it had been raining, in the winter, dark outside to drive me home instead of me waiting alone the 20 minutes for the bus in an almost deserted industrial estate. It had been weird, being in his car and he took a long time getting into the car to start driving. I had wondered if he was trying to make a move on me, I sat there silently and acted stupid because I was scared.

Not of Chris, who again could have easily overpowered me if he had wanted to. No, I feared Allan and what he would think. It was made worse by the fact that when driving me home, I told him the wrong street, and we got lost. It sounds unconvincing but I can absolutely promise nothing happened. I didn't like Chris that way and I just wanted to get home. I hated not being able to drive, that Allan didn't drive. That I had to rely on buses or taxis. I was cold and tired and just wanted to get home even though I never knew what I was going home to.

I had plenty of opportunities to cheat on him that I chose to ignore. I believed him when he said he never cheated on me. I know now that he cheated on me constantly and with anyone he could. "Both of those children are yours." The same thing I was repeating constantly to him, night after night.

"Well, I guess I can't really say my daughter isn't. She looks too much like me but our son? He doesn't look anything like me." Oh, what a fucking shame that one of my own children possibly might look like me. I did physically create them in my own body after all. Getting annoyed and snapping at him happened more often than I meant to, I couldn't keep myself together all the time.

"You know what, why don't we get a DNA test done? On both kids and that way when the results come back stating categorically that they are both yours, I will fucking frame the results and hang them on the living room wall. And you know what, if you fucking dare to even question it or bring it up again I can point at the results and remind you that you're a delusional, selfish fucking cunt."

It wasn't nice or polite, but I believe I made my point clear enough. I know the parentage of both of those children and not for one second did I believe that anyone else could be the father of either child. I knew it, absolutely without any doubt in my mind. Allan was the father to both. Asshole.

It would have been easier for me if he wasn't.

***

There was the incident when he went to Birmingham with work for an awards ceremony and decided that when he was there, all suited and booted, to send me selfies with the beautiful brunette he met and spent his time at the Awards Ceremony with.

Now, please remember that this man did not drink alcohol, he was not drunk when he did this. It wasn't a drunken accident. It was a calculated move; he did this deliberately to make me jealous or at least make me react.

She was beautiful, nothing like me but that didn't make me feel insecure. In fact, she looked a lot like his mother, and I believe I may have even responded saying so… I hope I did. She had long brown hair, was tall and thin. I wasn't jealous the way he wanted me to be, I didn't care if he found someone else. I actively hoped and prayed he would. Not to push the abuse onto someone else but so I could escape.

I believed that men leave their wives when they get older, they leave for younger women. That's what we were told in my generation growing up. So, I hoped that he would meet someone else and leave me for them. That since he was obviously so unhappy and told me every time he beat and raped me that it was my fault he did it, that he wouldn't do it to someone else (I'm just special, I guess). That he would be happier away from me.

That was my reasoning, so I allowed myself to hope that he would leave me for this woman in Birmingham and I could live my life in peace, with the kids and we'd be happier for it.

My marriage could not be saved, it was a sinking ship, the best thing we could both do was cut our losses before they got any worse.

It was just a shame that I realised only after the separation that he was perfectly happy as he was. He had everything, exactly the way he wanted it. That was unfathomable to me, because of how fucking miserable I was each day. That is unfortunately the reality, he had everything he ever wanted when we were together. If I had realised that sooner, maybe I would have left earlier.

***

I got into a habit early in the marriage saying, "we" instead of "me". It was a silly thing, it was always, "we did this," and rarely ever, "I did this." Even though it was normally only me who actively did anything. Even now, it's so ingrained in me that I still catch myself going to say, "we did this."

I haven't spoken to him directly in over six years. I sometimes find myself touching my ring finger and realising my wedding ring is no longer there and finding that both a comfort and not. I don't miss him, I'm not capable of missing anything about him. Those emotions are completely closed off to me now but it's a great example of emotional conditioning and how years together can be just as damaging because it's customary, it's what was normal.

He was in my life so much and now he's not. My life is better for it, always would be but part of me feels stuck back then with him, having never left. I feel like time stopped for me, I'm still in that house, and that another house with him.

There's that internet story going around about the lamp and how it looks different one day. The person wakes up to realise that they have imagined a whole life with a family that didn't exist and that's how I feel sometimes in reverse. Like I never really left. It's that shadow period in a horror movie, the calm before the storm. The reprieve before the grand finale. I'm always waiting for the curtain to fall, for the story to end and it just keeps going on and on without any conclusion in sight.

Not safe to be drunk or have fun around him

The audacity that men feel entitled to your body. How much power they have over you. I have excused men's shitty behaviour, and I have enabled men's shitty behaviour. I played the role of abuse apologiser, and I have allowed my husband to use me to gaslight others into believing he is one of the only good ones.

Sitting around the table, my huge husband overwhelmed me by his sheer size. I was smaller than normal at this stage, slim, with long dark hair which he hated. He had made sure to constantly tell me how much he hated it. It was always his way to make me go back to being blonde. He preferred me blonde; bleached like his teenage crush, the beautiful blonde superhero. He chose me because I looked like her.

Tanned and skinny were his other preferences, everything that I wasn't naturally. The tight fitted dress was a little big on me because I had been restricting what I had been eating, desperate to give him something less to shout at me for. I'd just get angry at him in return, and I knew all too well what he would do to me if I dared get angry at him.

The past few years I had slowly succumbed to bulimia, using laxatives to stop my stomach from looking bloated. I knew that laxatives didn't stop my body from absorbing the calories in any food I did eat. Long-term issues with eating disorders had left my stomach struggling to digest and expel any waste, so I constantly had painful bloating which blew my stomach up like a balloon. I'd look pregnant. I wasn't at the time very well educated around my body and even the effects that food and eating had on my monthly cycle or the impact that could have on how my body worked.

Another more insidious reason for the dependence on laxatives was the anal rape that Allan had started. He hurt me anally, deliberately and that made pooping an extremely painful experience.

I had said to him that he was the most homophobic homosexual I had ever met. I was convinced at this stage that he was truly gay, in love with his best friend and completely ashamed of himself for something he had no control over. I think his parents, and in particular his grandparents had such an incredibly negative influence over his thinking in regards with his self-worth for being gay or bisexual. Even fluid in his sexuality, none of it would have mattered or made a difference to me.

I remember his mum telling me that she thought he was gay because he never brought back any girls to the house, not in high school, not in college. This was said negatively. How she had been relieved when he had finally brought me home. He had told me that was because he was embarrassed by his parents and didn't want to introduce anyone to them. I had believed that at the age of 19 because I was gullible and didn't know any better. I didn't question what he said because at the time I had no reason to.

Over time I had seen the way he was with other men. He had openly told stories in front of not just me but boasted in front of his friends that he had played with his male friends in high school in what sounded to me to be sexual assault or even rape. The guys being the way they all were with one another shrugged their shoulders and said it was just "boys being boys." It sounded illegal to me, especially knowing what he was capable of.

I am bisexual. He regularly made fun of me for being bi, but he was never worried about me leaving him for a woman or being friends with a woman for that reason. He did worry about me being around men. He would also make the most homophobic and disgusting jokes and statements and follow it up with the good old excuse of "I can't be homophobic; I have gay best friends." He was right, and it made people, mainly me, stop pushing how disgusting what he said was because that always shut everyone up. Of course he can't mean it offensively, that would mean he was being derogative about his own best friends. He had two friends who were openly queer; Sarah and Gerald.

If Allan had told me he was gay, even if he had told me he was not attracted to me, like I already suspected, then I would have fully supported him. I would have told his parents and grandparents to fuck off if they didn't support him. I would have fought anyone who gave him any trouble. I offered to stay in the marriage with him, to be a solid unit for our family. I just asked that he stop hitting me and raping me. I offered to have threesomes with him and another man. He punched me & strangled me for even suggesting such a thing.

For the sake of our children, I would have gotten him whatever help he needed for his mental health and to deal with whatever trauma he clearly had because ultimately I was obsessed with him being a better person, not to save our marriage, nothing could save that, but so he could be a better father to those two children. They deserved a father who loved them and created a safe place to play, learn and grow. That is what they needed, not the man who opened his mouth and could make any of the three of us cry by just speaking. He was disgusting in every way imaginable.

I digress, the fact that he was so obsessed with anal sex and only wanted to rape me from behind made me convinced that he wasn't attracted to me, especially not sexually. He was never able to get an erection with me unless he did something violent. It made the fact that he raped me at all in any hole even more confusing to me because I couldn't figure out why he would rape me at all. I had heard so many times people say that men who rape can't control their urges. What was his urge then? He wasn't raping me because he was overcome with lust for me that he couldn't stop himself, couldn't control himself that he absolutely had to take me right then and there… It made no sense to me, none of it did.

Little did I realise that he was in control the whole time. It was never about rage or lust. If it had been, he would have raped me in public or in front of someone else. Every move he made was calculated because he only raped me when there were no witnesses.

This night was a horrible night too, it was a thirtieth birthday party for one of our friends, Artie. The birthday boy had rented a hall and put on a disco. It would have been good fun if fun wasn't something that Allan sucked out of me. I had been drinking a little but wasn't drunk. Allan had come over to the table I was sitting at. He had spent the evening wandering around everyone else and being his normal sociable self.

Eventually taking the seat beside me and talking mostly to Ryan who was sitting at the top of this table. Ryan was already quite drunk, and Allan was determined to make him more so. Challenging Ryan (the rapist as he was nicknamed in our friend group for good reason) to a drinking competition to down whole glasses of vodka. It was rare to see Allan drink alcohol at all, but he downed it with barely any effect. Ryan on the other hand was having a hard time taking in the alcohol, swaying from side to side as he tried to keep up with Allan.

I had a bad feeling about this. Ryan disgusted me after his behaviour those years previously, I had never looked at him the same again. I was worried about his behaviour after drinking so much. I was right to be concerned.

It wasn't until we were leaving, Allan had gone outside to wait for our taxi that Ryan decided to try and hug me goodbye. He was drunk, and he grabbed me, and I tried to endure it. Until he placed his hand on my crotch and tried to rub my vagina through my dress.

I froze, which I have realised is what I do whenever someone sexually assaults or rapes me for the first time. I stood there, backing off from the hug and staring at him in disgust. He said something horribly suggestive to me, leering in a creepy way. I ran away from him, out of the hall and outside to Allan.

Of course I ran to the man I thought would protect me. I was terrified to tell him because I was convinced he would have accused me of leading Ryan on or doing something to deserve it. I was afraid he wouldn't understand since he rarely did. He blamed me for everything, and as such, I usually blamed myself.

Scared to tell him but traumatised by what had happened, I spoke to him and explained exactly what Ryan had done. He looked at me in a way I found hard to understand, he didn't react at all. He just said, "ok," and never said anything about it again.

It confused me.

Wasn't he supposed to protect me? Wasn't he going to at the very least tell Ryan off for having touched me like that? Wasn't he going to say or do something? As far as I am aware, he never did anything.

I finally realised then that he didn't care enough about me to protect me.

Book and movies

The only thing we truly bonded over was a love of stories. He was obsessed with everything from the big screen to the small screen. Some genuinely good times we had were going to movies, special screenings or anniversary screenings together. He also shared my love for musicals.

At one point he made me go see every single film that came out at the cinema. He pushed me to be overwhelmed from the sensory aspect and never getting time in between to recover to then be dragged to something else equally as over stimulating.

He took me to see A Star Is Born because I love Lady Gaga, taking me to a meal beforehand and knowing I was actively suicidal at the time, let me watch that movie. He knew the full plot and ending because he always investigated movies beforehand. Allan was pissed off afterwards when I was stunned into silence for two days due to the suicide of one of the main characters. When he took me home, he told me he expected sex (not rape, consensual sex where I was expected to actively participate) after putting on such a nice night for me. I was in shock.

The existentialism of such suicides is what is triggering for me, or it used to be, I've gone past desensitised now. The fact that Bradley Cooper's character was trying so hard to get better, and that one little thing set him off. I knew that feeling, deeply. I had been there so many times myself.

When Thirteen Reasons Why season one came out, he was obsessed with it. He stayed up through the night it aired and watched it all in one go. Again, I was actively suicidal, barely holding on at the time. He begged and demanded that I watch it too, with him. I had seen the information online about how the main character kills herself in the original scenes before it was changed. That kind of suicide, it is how I had tried it when I was younger, it was extremely triggering for me. He went on about it constantly for weeks. Eventually, we compromised because I fucking refused to watch the TV show, was that he bought me the book to read. Which I did, while I was in bed, being so depressed I was struggling to get out of bed at all at that point in my life.

Ironically, the book encouraged me to think up a story, my own version of Thirteen Reasons Why based on my own experiences of feeling suicidal. It gave me a new, welcomed perspective around wanting to kill myself. That other people were to blame for it, not me. I was reacting to my environment. The abuse, the unsafe situations that other people were putting me into, were causing me to feel so depressed and a hopelessness that made me feel like my death was the only escape.

It reminded me of a conversation I'd had with a GP while suffering from post-partum depression. I'd explained how I was feeling to the doctor, who had known me since I was a child. His advice stuck with me and was more truthful than I could accept at the time. He said, "no number of pills will make you feel better if you are unhappy in your life, your job and marriage." I had wanted a pill to make me feel normal, to be like everyone else. I was obsessed with "fixing myself."

When I went home, I told Allan about this conversation. He too had wanted me to be medicated, to make me a "normal woman." When he heard the doctor's advice, he was angry. Convinced that they were going to convince me to leave him, and as such I was not allowed to go to the doctors again. I was only allowed if he was there with me.

Then there is one of his favourite TV shows, the Walking Dead. How he used my fear of zombies to force me to watch that TV show knowing how scared it made me? How he'd laugh at me for being afraid. Or how when Negan came onto the show, that he started using the characters catch phrases and trying to put on his accent while he was raping me. How much it triggers me even now, brings me right back to those moments with Allan of, "Look at you, taking it like a champ!" He bought himself a replica of Lucille, and would walk around the house knocking on various doors and singing, "Little pigs, little pigs..."

One of the last things we watched together in the old house was the anime Toky Ghoul. There is a torture scene the main charcater goes through and the one torturing him, tells him about his own experiences with such things. He tells him to do maths in his head to help endure pain. It's the sum of starting at 1000 and subtracting 7 and see if you can get to zero. Once we moved, Allan started while raping me, telling me to do 1000-7. While raping me, he would ask how far I'd get and what number I was now on. He would verbally encourage me while raping me. One time I made it all the way into the 400's but I lost track and had to start back at 1000.

An interesting fact about me, I absolutely suck at simple maths equations. I regularly muddle up numbers in sequence and struggle with any adding or subtracting that includes the number 7 or 8. I am good at writing, reading and used to be great at speaking but maths was always something I struggled with. I have ADHD so keeping my focus on anything is difficult, especially something I'm not good at. Doing that in my head, really helped me not focus as much on what was happening to me physically.

I suppose the one and only credit I can really give him is he got me back into reading. Although he had mocked me for attending university to study English and laughed at my ambitions to become a fiction writer, he did buy me books, and lots of them. He even at one stage bought me a laptop and verbally encouraged me to write stories. Then he got paranoid that I was writing about him, didn't allow me to have any passwords on said laptop and mocked me for anything I did write. I gave up. In a way I think he tried to connect with me, not for genuine love but to make me believe that he loved me and solidify the belief that someone so wonderfully generous and creative could never be a man who raped his wife.

He would buy me the books which were turned into movies or tv shows that he was interested in watching. I will say this for him, for all the bad parts and those are astounding in volume, the one thing he did do right was pick books for me. A lot of my favourites were ones that he had bought me, even against my will because I was wilful and stubborn, refusing gifts from him because they always had strings attached. I always enjoyed the stories and the subsequent movies that we would go and watch together.

I was desperate for not only love but friendship & connection.

He also used this to ruin every major story line. He would research the books, find out key plots and cliffhangers and tell me them just as I was about to get to them. It always took away the feeling of excitement while reading. He'd loan out my books without permission but refuse anyone to borrow his own DVDs. Everything was a double standard, if I had ruined an ending to a movie for him, he'd have beaten me for it. It was that important to him.

She knows what her grandson is really like

Sitting in the parked car, a small white thing, outside of the postal depot I had listened to Jennifer moan and complain about her grandson the entire trip. One of the many downsides to not being able to drive myself, having to rely on other people. These kinds of interactions were always difficult for me.

"He's such an asshole, the way he speaks to me, his grandad, to his mum, and his dad, it's disgusting!" She was genuinely upset with him, he had phoned the day before as usual and caused a massive argument probably because he had been bored. Anytime something had happened the first thing he did was phone her, then Richard, then Natalie and then Derek. He didn't bother speaking to me about anything, he never valued my opinion. Clearly, he didn't think I was intelligent enough to understand or experienced enough to give any decent advice that was worth him listening to.

Maybe the problem was that I was more intelligent than him and he didn't like to give me the place I deserved in our marriage as an equal partner. He admitted sometimes that he knew I was smarter. Was that why he shut me out of everything? He needed someone to feed his ego, not give him logical advice. God, forgive I wanted to be involved in our finances, or anything that was important to us both.

I let her rant and rave about him, knowing it was better she slag him off to me and not phone him to tell him what an awful person he was. Still, it was a strain on my mental health, my patience has never been the best. I turned to her and said, "Well, he only speaks to you like that sometimes, that's how he speaks to me and the kids all the time." That shut her up. I got out of the car and went into the depot to collect the parcel.

Furious

"I've decided not to kill you off now." Unexpectedly, in the middle of doing something, he would come out with the most unbelievable nonsense. This was in relation to his story that he wanted to script, film and make into a TV show. It had been his lifelong ambition to become a famous director, after wanting to be a marine biologist when he was a child. He had rarely shown ambition with action, but he liked to talk a lot.

In this story, which was mostly contained inside his head, he had built the main character around himself and it was about him while he was still in high school (the time in life that he constantly liked to remind me, was his favourite and everything had been downhill since then…) with his friends taking on the local crime lord and essentially going to war with them. It was a basic story, mainly good versus evil with a lot of casualties along the way. He had a wildly active imagination and spent a lot of time in his head, fine tuning the details. As far as I'm aware he never actually put pen to paper and wrote any of it down, but it kept him busy and out of my way.

I never saw anything wrong with this type of maladaptive daydreaming because I did it too. It was my coping mechanism since I was a child and what I used to write, wanted to use to create gigantic worlds of magic that one day I would write an epic fantasy series. Hint said fantasy series will be coming out in the future because I've spent the last five years working on and off on it! I have a constant internal monologue, and this is what I use to write with.

I left him to his daydreams and didn't get shocked about how he went back and forth from me, being the lead characters love interest, would sometimes be raped, sometimes murdered, sometimes tortured because it was all for story and character development. It didn't worry me or shock me too much at the time. I had a very real danger to contend with; a fantasy world barely registered in my head.

It wasn't until I got into listening to true crime podcasts some years later and realised that this was a common theme in serial killers. They would invent worlds in their imaginations where they would daydream specifically about torturing, raping and killing people. Usually, it was based on a specific person they knew, like a mother or wife. Not just some made up character. This leads to acting out these fantasies in later life. This sounded suspiciously like what Allan had been doing.

The difference with me, is I wasn't thinking specifically about killing anyone. I would use this to create actual plots and worldbuilding. It was storytelling and creation. He had been fantasising about raping, torturing and murdering me.

Most times after he had raped me, that anger, that freak adrenaline rush made me believe in those moments after he had violently, sexually violated me, that I could harm him. That feeling always vanished quickly, turning into melancholy as I would lose a piece of me repeatedly, each time leaving me with less ability to want to do anything, let alone hurt even him.

For him though, he would randomly come out with new plot points, sometimes asking things like, "Would you prefer to have both your legs, or both your arms amputated?" He had been sitting there imagining both my legs being severed from my body and how much "stronger" that would make me, more grateful for life surviving such torture. I'd tell him neither, that I'd like to keep my arms and legs. He'd later say something like, "I decided to remove both your arms AND legs." Maybe he was trying to get a reaction out of me, maybe he was trying to frighten me but even now it feels weird and unsettling.

He had a fantasy within this world of ending the series with his death. The final scene was of everyone (and he meant crowds of people, so many people there's not enough room for them all) standing around his coffin, at his funeral, celebrating his life. This main character had given his life to save the others in a bold act of love, the greatest sacrifice. He felt that was the best way to go.

He'd tell me about how my character would be standing there or was perhaps in a wheelchair after being raped and tortured by these "gang mafia types" crying, so sad that he was dead. Proud of him giving up his life to save everyone. He even paired me up romantically with his best friend, having asked him to take care of me in the event of his death.

I kept telling him he was too selfish to sacrifice himself for someone else.

AUGUST 2016

If I felt that my life was falling apart, I would have been right regardless of how much denial I kept myself living in. The month of August 2016 is branded deep into my skin by the actions of my ex-husband during this time. For the weekends of THAT August were the centre of the worst violence I had up to that point, ever known in my life. This set the standard for what was to be the final three years with him.

What scared me the most those days were the fact that it was unlike anything I had experienced before, with anyone, especially not him. The anger that exploded out of Allan felt homicidal as if it was taking every ounce of self-control he had not to kill me. It was rage, dark and swirling with horror which struck a fear inside me I couldn't grasp. Being afraid of Allan was something I was used to. Being in a situation where he could have easily killed me was something I was used to. This was something completely different, an unhinged side to him I hadn't even known possible.

It started almost immediately when he came home from work on the first Friday evening. He didn't care anymore about the usual things like me having his dinner ready and waiting for him or even pretending to be civil in front of the kids. He would almost immediately grab me and drag me from whatever room I was in at the time and take me to a room furthest away from the kids.

In doing this he would bang my head off the doorframe or banister in the struggle of him dragging me as I tried to escape. He was under the impression that they couldn't hear any of the noise but that was ignorance on both our parts. I learned to my grave horror later that the children heard every word, every cry for help and were unable to do anything to help, blaming themselves for not being able to intervene with what their father was choosing to do.

And it was a choice. Never be fooled into thinking that a man's actions are the result of drugs, alcohol or some other addiction or mental affliction. It is a choice and as women, we are more easily manipulated into feeling sorry for them and therefore forgiving them when there is something to blame. Oh, it's not his fault, he loves me. No, fortunately he doesn't love you, any more than my ex-husband loved me. It wasn't in his nature to love or understand what love is. But he knows that you do and that is the weapon which is wielded against you and instrumental in keeping you quiet about it.

It is my genuine belief that Allan never loved me, I don't think he even liked me. I believe he absolutely fucking hated me. I have no idea why. I struggle to understand marrying someone, choosing to stay in a relationship with someone you absolutely hate? I had no choice but to stay with him despite hating him for the abuse he forced me to endure. He had every choice and option at his disposal and he chose to stay.

I also don't know what it was about me that he hated?

The whole time I couldn't help but think what did I do to deserve this?

The next day I remember him pinning me to the bed and screaming in my face. The words are lost to me now, but the absolute rage and hatred that he shouted at me still make my ears ring. I kept wondering exactly what I had done wrong to cause such a reaction in him. What had happened because of how angry he was with me.

I genuinely had no idea then and less of an idea now.

He spat on me. I can't say that I haven't spat at him when the situation was reversed. In his wedding speech he talked about how one of the first days we had worked together in Blockbuster I had spat a mouthful of Fanta orange juice at him on a dare. No one found it funny, but he did, he was always intrigued by my weird quirks and my inability to refuse a dare or be out done. I had spat at him many times while he had me pinned on my back trying to rape me, I had done it to discourage him from continuing. It's not a nice thing, certainly not how he spat at me in disgust.

He seemed disgusted by me. I couldn't figure out what I had done to cause him to be disgusted at me like that?

Side note: I don't think now that this had anything to do with me. Allan always used violence against me, as a way of being violent towards himself. He used me like a mirror in this regard, dishing out the punishment on me physically that he felt he deserved himself. This was a projection. I hadn't done anything wrong, nothing that deserved this reaction. So, it does make me wonder what he had done to cause himself to react like this about something he was obviously feeling guilty about. I have my theories but that's not my story to tell.

He screamed, he spat on me, he shook me viciously. He hit me, slapped me, punched me repeatedly for hours. This continued for the best part of a morning and afternoon. He raped me repeatedly and I was numb, stuck there, terrified and unsure of what was going to happen next. This was one of many times, I felt like he was going to kill me.

Eventually, he stopped, and he moved off me and away from the bed, sitting down on a chair. He was leaned over, silent, head in both hands and he just sat there. I was still lying on my back, covered in his spit and come. There was blood everywhere and I knew I had wet myself. I was lying in a puddle and felt mortified. I felt dirty and disgusting. I hadn't even had time to shower or bathe in the morning, so I was sweaty and felt sore everywhere.

The Saturday morning had turned into Saturday afternoon, and for now it seemed to have stopped.

I stood on wobbly legs, my feet unable to be flat against the carpet. I shuffled, terrified to make any sudden movements. He hadn't given me permission to leave the room, but he was sitting down, head in his hands, he had battered me so badly and for so long that he had exhausted himself and he needed to rest. Every part of me hurt, the pain was widespread and everywhere.

My head was banging, pounding from the sobbing and the knocks I had already taken. I carefully tried to wipe away the saliva and blood from my face. I tried not to make any sudden movements because I didn't want to anger him, I didn't want to upset him. I was scared, but in my head, I felt that if I can make it to the bathroom, if I can clean up a little then maybe, I could escape this whole incident with my mental health intact.

I was desperately trying to cling onto some sanity, have a little control in a wildly ridiculous situation that was out of my control. I didn't want him to see me move, frightened of what he would do to me next but at the same time I was only going to the bathroom. I needed the toilet despite wetting myself already which was embarrassing enough but I also needed to clean the come from me. I needed it off me, it was burning into my skin and screaming at me. I wanted a bath more than anything but that might be too ambitious right now. Besides, a part of me wondered if he would try and drown me in it.

I just wanted to go to the toilet, I shuffled my feet along, I was covered in bruises already. Not to mention the urine I had been forced to lie in. It took everything in me to not cry out loud, sob loudly and ugly at what he had done to me. Why, I couldn't figure out why. I was moving so slowly, it was a short distance from the bedroom to the bathroom, barely any distance at all. As I was getting closer, I heard him coming after me. He was angry, I could tell from how fast he was moving, shouting, "NO," as I walked so slowly. What on earth could he be angry at me for now.

He grabbed me by the hair, a massive tangle in his fist and threw me forward. The force of which he did meant I was thrown into the bathroom. I went forward, falling towards the toilet and did so with such force that my forehead banged off the cistern of the toilet and as I fell, the side of my head then banged against the heavy tile on the wall.

There was a small gap between the toilet and the wall, and I fell in between there. Later we would discover there was a leak in the toilet, as he had thrown me with such force it had moved the toilet itself. My head hurt and I lay on the floor curled on my side.

The anger in him was nothing I had ever seen, least of all directed towards me. There was a complete attitude change this first weekend and it would only get worse from here.

He stood over me, towering above me, his height and sheer size blocking out everything else. I was crying softly and my chest heaving in panic. He started screaming words at me, incomprehensible as I could not distinguish anything he was saying. Screaming, shouting, angry, spitting as he screamed at me.

He began kicking me in the stomach as he swore and called me every name you could think of. This man, who would tell me he loved me, was kicking me repeatedly in the stomach and then the back. I thought I was going to die, right there, on the bathroom floor. I thought about my body being discovered, in such a vile state that I'd be a laughingstock. No one would take me seriously. Dear Allan and his whore-wife. I wished at that moment I had done any of the things he had accused me of because in my head, it would at least make sense as to why he was attacking me, why he hated me so badly. What had I done to deserve this? Why was this happening to me? Why?

Eventually it was over. As it was already afternoon and none of us had eaten much, he decided to order in pizza for delivery. He was always his most generous in these moments. He told me to get in the bath and get cleaned up, making sure to take my mobile phone. I had on occasion threatened to call the police afterwards, he would take my phone away from me until I had "calmed down."

***

Later, as the kids went to bed, it started up again. This time in the living room, he beat me with the same ferocity as he had earlier in the day. He strangled me and punched me, slapping me repeatedly.

Eventually, it was around 1am and he had stopped, sitting down on the large corner sofa we had. I sat at the opposite end; we could see each other. I decided to speak to him. No bullshit, no sugar coating, just direct communication because what the fuck did it matter anymore? I had been so long in denial about what was happening, what he was doing and blaming myself. I decided to just speak to him, tell him exactly how I felt and how it affected me. Ask him what the fuck was happening? I hoped he would see how bad things had gotten and how we needed to separate. This could not continue.

I wished I had died rather than endure anything that happened this month. The existential dread of knowing that what started this month, would continue for three years. Well, two years and 11 months.

I thought I knew the violence men were capable of and yet, he surprised me this month with how badly it became.

He spent the Friday evenings, most of Saturday, most of Sunday and the Monday mornings brutally and violently attacking and raping me. Each weekend was the same, minus the alternating weekends I worked as a carer overnight. For me, it really did start with no warning. This was unusual even for him. That's what shocked me the most, was the absolute and utter change in him. It was, however, how things only amplified and got worse from here. He did things to me he had never done before or took things he did regularly and somehow made them worse.

This month broke me. If ever I died, it would have been this month because the events left me devoid of a lot. Something changed within me fundamentally, especially early this one Sunday morning when he did something after I expressly said that the one thing I couldn't take happening to me anymore... My whole self-collapsed in on itself and part of me, never recovered from this one incident when I was left on a cold wooden floor in a puddle of my own making, mixed with my own blood, left to lie there unable to pick myself up.

This would have been a great time for a hero to come in and rescue me. This was one of many times where I couldn't, more importantly, did not want to live through. I spoke to God that night, like I had started to and asked him not to let me wake up in the morning. That I was done with life and just wanted to pass away in my sleep. I didn't want to wake up and yet, I woke up because I'm still here today.

I am not grateful for that.

If I could go back in time, I would give that girl the biggest hug because she needed it. What a difference some kind words from someone, a hug would have made to her then. She needed a hero and honestly, I don't like the whole she had to save herself nonsense because what the fuck are other people for if not for helping when you're in need?

Hyper independence is a trauma response I have mastered not because I don't ask for help when I need it but because despite myself, I learned to ask for her to never actually get any help. I have been let down time after time, so honestly, what is the point in there being over 8 billion people in the world if not even one of them helped me when I was desperately in need of help?

***

I said to him, "I can't do this anymore, I won't…"

I spoke to him more honestly that night than I ever did at any other time. I was worn out, the fight gone but I spoke calmly, logically and from the heart. I told him I was done; I was thirty now and my body couldn't handle the physical fighting the same as I could in my twenties. I didn't want this; I didn't want this to be my life. I hated that he hit me, I hated that he raped me.

I told him specifically that the worst thing he ever did to me, the pain and the emotional damage was unbearable SPECIFICALLY when he raped me anally that I could not cope and struggled to come back from it. I told him I wanted the marriage to end, that I couldn't understand why he didn't also want it to end. That we should separate, go our separate ways and move on. That we would be better friends, better parents for it.

And then he did what broke my heart more than anything else.

I think what broke my heart the most was that I had literally said the words out loud to him just moments before and because I had told him my weakness, he chose in that moment to do that exact thing and for that reason.

I knew, I knew as soon as he stood, even before he grabbed me, dragging me to the edge of the sofa and bent me over it.

I had told him that this was the worst thing he had ever done to me, I had been vulnerable, I had told him my weakness and he absolutely, in this moment, chose to exploit that.

He held me down, I immediately started crying, but he pushed my face against the thick black leather of the sofa, and he roughly pulled down whatever trousers I was wearing. Legging, pjs, I can't remember and I'm confident they went in the bin afterwards along with all my clothes. He rarely used lube or any spit or any kind of help when he raped me anally.

He wasn't trying to go near my vagina; his intention was deliberate. He raped me anally from behind, that couch was unfortunately a perfect size for being able to angle me at his height and keep me suffocated against the leather cushion. I cried.

I didn't shout, I didn't push him off, I wasn't physically able at that time. He knew because I had verbally expressed how this made me feel physically and emotionally and he did this to me deliberately.

He would also going forward be able to use raping me anally as a scare tactic when I was fighting him raping me vaginally or orally. "If you don't let me do this, I'll stick it in your ass," is what he would say to threaten me. That would usually make me comply because I was so scared of the damage, the pain of him raping me anally. It was physically but not emotionally easier to relent and try to just let him finish quickly.

He raped me and he broke my heart for the last time that night.

After he was done, he just left me there, didn't even look back before walking out the room and going off to his bed where I'm sure he fell asleep with a smile on his face, no doubt extremely pleased with himself.

I stayed stuck there for a few moments before I slipped down from the couch and lay on the floor. I was bloody, had pissed myself, had his come running out my ass and all over my thighs with tears and snot covering my face.

I just lay there for a while.

I wanted to die.

Nothing was ever the same after that night.

The colour was leached from the world; I lost sight of everything that I cared about or that mattered to me. I chopped my hair off, made myself as "ugly" as possible. Gained a lot of weight, stopped wearing any nice clothes and started giving up on wearing makeup. Everything became a chore, everything became difficult. My whole body routinely hurt, and my head never cleared properly again.

    I have never been the same since that one night in August 2016.

The following month

One memory I have that I do almost laugh at was after we both started the new jobs at the local council, we both had a training session together in the September. It was a domestic abuse training session as part of the role we did, this later went against me in court, was helping victims of domestic abuse find housing, financial support etc.

The session was held by a woman, and I'm annoyed I can't remember her name; I was too shocked for it to sink in. She had been a teacher, went into law enforcement and as such now went around teaching and educating workplaces, the police etc. Anyone who was front line in working with those experiencing domestic abuse.

The irony was that Allan and I, sat together at a school style desk, just the two of us, side by side in front of the group together. She did her deeply probing and brutally honest presentation of exactly what domestic abuse is. We sat there, even watching the video she showed everyone and listened to the whole presentation. It was one of the most eye opening but awkward moments of my life.

There was no place for denial now.

Afterwards there was a table set up with brochures and brooches, the white ribbon for violence against women. They were for us to wear at work to show we support domestic abuse victims. I took a pin and attached it to my lanyard and wore it with pride the next few years. I lost that one when I eventually moved out but I ordered myself a new one online so I could continue to wear it at work. Wearing that little white ribbon made me feel like I was being brave even when I didn't feel I was brave at all.

We both left with everyone else. I got into his car (due to this job and his location being out of the town we stayed in, he had gotten driving lessons, finally passing his test which meant we had our own car for the first time) and he drove away from the City office back to Hometown. Just outside of City, he pulled the car into a side stop area and shut off the car.

After the presentation I had a bigger sense of dread because I was struck by my situation and how bad it was. How I could no longer lie to myself about the very real danger I was in. Denial is its own safety net. She had gone into detail about what it meant when someone strangles you. Not to be confused with choking because choking is when you choke on a piece of food. Strangulation is when someone puts their hands on your throat with the intention to hurt you. Strangulation is an act that precedes murder.

She even gave statistics of how many times strangulation comes before murder.

I should be dead.

It is that serious.

If someone has strangled you, run.

I had been experiencing this for years already from him, and had shrugged my shoulders to myself, making myself minimise the seriousness of the situation which was as bad as it could be.

Right now, in this car, with him stopping and feeling the energy that was rolling off him, I sat there and thought, "he is going to kill me, this is it." Instead of killing me, he said things that froze my blood within my veins and terrified me more than if he had actually tried.

He acknowledged that he was a rapist.

He acknowledged that he was a domestic abuser.

He said he knew what he did to me and couldn't lie or hide it anymore.

It was a strange lucid period of truth from him, something I wasn't used to him being with me. Mostly everything was a performance of some sort and yet, this felt genuine. It scared me more than anything else and although I had wanted him to admit it. Hearing him admit it out loud was worse.

He knew and he did it anyway.

He knew and he cared, but not enough to change or let me go.

I was stuck with a fucking madman who would turn on me at any moment. What's worse is he enjoyed it.

Sexualised to the point of not being able to do normal activities without inspiring rape

I wasn't able to do an at home yoga video without him panting and masturbating at the back of me, watching me, wanting to just fuck me against my will. I wasn't able to exercise; I couldn't do any aerobics or dancing. I couldn't do anything that involved me jumping up and down because my massive breasts bounced too much and apparently that was me teasing him. Bending, stretching, moving around on the floor, there's no position or stance that he didn't sexualise somehow.

I couldn't wear tight clothes because that's teasing him, I couldn't walk around wearing just a baggy t-shirt and pants because that's teasing him. I couldn't wear makeup, not wear makeup… He would say I should be grateful that after two kids that he even wants to fuck me at all… That he doesn't care about all my imperfections.

I didn't think of them as imperfections and thought he was a malicious cunt for even suggesting such a thing but whatever. I couldn't wear dresses, I couldn't wear nighties, I couldn't wear anything sexy at all because everything turned him on. He was insatiable, watching porn at all hours of the day, masturbating up to eight times a day and coming in his socks, his boxers. He used his shirt, jumper or t-shirt to clean up the mess a few times and then dumped all this stuff around the house; on the couch, the floor, wherever.

He was revolting and he disgusted me. The thought of him or anyone else touching me made me feel physically sick. I didn't even want people touching me affectionately or in passing. Everyone seemed to feel entitled to my body, never asking for permission and placing their hands on me. My body, my arm, my hair. It made me want to scrub the very skin of my bones, bleach it and burn it off… I hadn't self-harmed in so long but the urge to carve him out of me was overwhelming.

I couldn't even dye my hair at home without him sexualising it. The motion of shaking the bottle, to combine the formula, looked too much like a hand-job for him. I had to stop doing these things in front of him. How difficult he made day to day tasks, how unenjoyable and dreaded these things became.

MY LAST SUICIDE ATTEMPT

Because of course, even I would fail at trying to kill myself.

I can't do anything right.

Sometimes Allan hurt me, and it surprised me. Sometimes Allan hurt me, and he got freaked out that he had hurt me. The compassion and empathy felt real even though I knew it wasn't. I didn't trust it and it confused me.

I learned that sometimes if I hurt myself then he would panic and stop harming me. This was one of those times.

The previous month I had been trying to paint a bit of the kitchen ceiling. Me being me, and unable to do anything safely or correctly because I had no value in my own safety, I did this by climbing up on a dining chair. I successfully fixed the bit of painting and decided to jump down from the chair onto the floor.

Now, enter my issues with hypermobility and how fucked up my joints are. Also, add in the previous injury I had as a child and broke the toes on my right foot when I was ten years old. What happened was a crunch and a break in the bone of my big toe. It hurt, and since it was night,

I didn't want to cause any scene by asking to be taken to the hospital. So, I went to bed with the intention of seeing how it would be in the morning.

The next morning the foot was bruised and more painful than it had been the night before. Normally Allan wouldn't have taken me to the hospital but even he recommended that I get it checked out and he took the morning off work to take me as I went to get an X-ray. He did however complain about it the whole way of course, telling me how inconvenient it was and how much of a hassle I am. After a few hours in the hospital, mostly waiting around, the X-ray confirmed the small break in my toe, and I was recommended to stay off the foot to let it heal.

After a short visit to his grandparents on our way back home, because he could never take me straight home, Jennifer offered me a full box of co-codamol which she received in bulk from her GP for pain. The box hadn't been opened, and I kept it in the kitchen only using the odd one or two as I am usually too forgetful to take medicine. The ADHD diagnosis came out of nowhere later in life of course.

Suicide is always on my mind. It's the one constant that has always been with me throughout my life. It's almost a comfort in some ways. The slightest inconvenience and the idea presents itself inside my mind, you should just kill yourself. I imagine the voice as a preppy cheerleader, waving shimmering pom poms of rainbows and shades of pink. Maybe a little silver or holographic added in for a little extra fun. The idea starts off small and I can usually ignore it, push it away and remind myself that there are things in life to be grateful for...

But what is there to be grateful for?

That's how the tumble begins, the ideas build and magnify as the voice adds doubt to all the things I try to tell myself. The negative always wins, it always outshines the positive.

Imagine how quiet it would be? How peaceful and silent. Imagine how wonderful it would be not having to live with how bright the sounds are and how loud the colours are. Imagine this all just ends, no more pain, no more crying, no more deep, dark emptiness, no more desperation, no more having to try. Death might have been my best option, the only option truly available to me then.

He had hit me repeatedly, screaming at me and laughing as he hurt me. Allan had grabbed me and bent me over the sofa, raping me anally as I kicked and thrashed my body around trying to get him off me. He was too big and had me held too tightly. The pain was excruciating, causing me to cry out, sobbing uncontrollably as I tried to be quiet but was in such a state of distress and panic that I couldn't control the shaking and hyperventilating as I could only endure another incident with him.

After he had finished, ejaculating inside my ass and all over the back end of me, I felt dirty and violated. A feeling I was becoming accustomed to as just a normal part of my day-to-day life. I had wanted to die for a long time but immediately after he had let me go, I got up and walked through to the kitchen. Running the cold water tap I thought about my plan and how best to execute it. It was not premeditated; I took an opportunity presented to me.

I reached up and brought down the box. I opened it on the counter and started bursting the individual tablets from the blister pack one by one. I had taken an overdose accidentally (honestly) when I was 15 years old and it had taken me years to be able to get over the psychological scarring left by taking so many pills at once. It left me physically unable to swallow tablets for years. Of course, this was now 16 years later, and I didn't have the same problem anymore.

I was conscious that Allan was sitting in the living room and normally didn't leave me alone after he had attacked me. I had threatened to do many things in the past including jumping out of the first floor kitchen window. He always aired on the side of caution just in case I chose to make a scene, exposing him. One by one I put the pills into my mouth, taking gulps of cold water as I tried to swallow them. I didn't get far, I only managed around 10 tablets before I felt his hand on my shoulder, his fingers digging into my skin as he spun me around to get a better look at what I was doing.

There was a strange mix of concern and anger on his face as he realised what I had done. He panicked, grabbing me and forcing me onto the floor on my back. I laughed at myself thinking, that was a stupid thing to do if he was trying to save me. His fingers forced his way into my throat and down as far as he could, his hands were big, and he was choking me.

An interesting thing about me is that I have a major gag reflex. It's ridiculous and annoying because although the reflex works, I have never been able to be sick in that way. It was inconvenient in my earlier disordered eating days as I realised, I was unable to make myself throw up, ever. I have emetophobia which again, psychologically shuts down the function of my throat despite me gagging, retching and choking. It's the worst.

Not so fun fact about me, having emetophobia is due to being intentionally poisoned by my gran. This was a deliberate act of Munchhausen by proxy, so as a child I was constantly vomiting. It was a running joke that I never tasted Christmas dinner properly until I was around 12 because she would intentionally make me sick for Christmas. When I was twelve, after throwing up in their bathroom sink, I remember, with absolute clarity thinking, this isn't something I should be used to. This isn't normal. Something psychological broke in my brain that day because ever since then I cannot vomit on my own.

I was a teenage anorexic, I tried to be bulimic so I know for a fact that I cannot, no matter how many fingers or implements I tried to stick down my throat, I would not throw up. I can only be sick when I either have a bug that renders me unable to keep the vomit down, or if I'm drunk enough that it bypasses the psychological issue, that keeps control firmly in place.

I had to try and explain this as I was now panicking, gagging and dry retching with zero ability to bring the tablets back up. He was aware of my struggles with this. He was trying to save my life and was also panicking, not listening to reason. I could never understand his reaction here; would it have been too difficult to explain to others why I had died? Why would I, his insane but darling wife, want to kill herself?

I lay there with his body weight crushing me and his dirty fingers choking me knowing he would do more harm than good. Eventually he stopped and asked me, "How many did you take?" He demanded angrily, practically screaming at me. "Not enough," I spluttered, already feeling sleepy, from not only the trauma of the rape but also the effect of the tablets.

I knew I would be ok; I hadn't taken enough to do any damage. "It's not enough, it wasn't enough." One thing I struggled to admit is that I have spent my life hiding addictions to pain killers, medications and alcohol. I knew my limits, I knew what my body could and could not take. Also, as I said earlier, this wasn't my first overdose.

He was calming down a little, unsure if this was just another trick, the fantasy he had of me was that I was some evil mastermind. Maybe that was a compliment from him. "You should go to the hospital; we need to get you to the hospital." It would have been endearing but I didn't trust it, why did he care? Allan wasn't capable of feeling anything towards me except anger and disgust, so what was the motivation here? "I'll be ok, if you take me to the hospital, they might section me."

That got the reaction I needed, truthfully, I was terrified to go to the hospital. We both knew that me saying that I had tried to kill myself would have consequences. The doctors would start asking me questions and in such an emotional state I couldn't be trusted not to tell the truth. I couldn't lie about something like this, not with the effect the tablets had on me. So, the hospital was out of the question. He instantly agreed, seeing reason and not wanting to risk being discovered as an abusive bastard.

"Are you going to be ok?" He stared at me as I moved back towards the living room, feeling weak and dizzy. I knew I'd fall unconscious soon. "I just need to nap, to sleep it off." His eyes narrowed, suddenly not trusting me. "I need to let this come out of my system, I'll be fine, I just need sleep." I felt my eyes closing, slurring my words as I lay down on the opposite end of the couch from where he had raped me. I closed my eyes involuntarily as I felt my head pounding. Hopefully I would die and hopefully I would never wake up, but I wasn't so lucky. I saw my daughter coming into the living room, happily bouncing about as my eyes closed and I hoped we'd be ok.

I demanded to go to the doctor a few days later telling him I was actively suicidal and wanted to die, that I needed some medication or else I was going to throw myself off the local bridge. Or throw myself in front of a bus or something because I would find a way out.

***

My mother used to always say that Louise is the smartest, dumbest person you'll ever meet and somehow, I feel as though the joke might still be on me. Does everyone know something I don't? That's how it feels.

Being in that abusive relationship is what I'd imagine being abducted and held against my will would feel like. I felt like I was being held hostage, I was not allowed to make the choice to leave. I told him repeatedly and I meant it, that I did not want to be in a relationship with him, he said no to me leaving. He said no when I asked him to leave. I tried to leave many times, and he physically stopped me every time. I would tell him that I didn't love him, I meant it but then he would strangle me or hit me until I agreed to take it back. I learned that I could take up to 15 punches to the face before relenting, saying anything he wanted to hear to make him stop.

Those stories you hear of men, usually kidnapping children or young women and hiding them away somewhere like an underground dungeon, keeping them imprisoned for years, decades sometimes. I get the feeling that comparison won't go down well with some people, making me out to be comparing my suffering to that of someone else who suffered more but I'd say it's the same situation.

The only difference is my captor allowed me outside, he dangled me in front of everyone for show, but I was still trapped. The threat of physical and sexual violence a keen influence in keeping me quiet, assuring my silence and obedience. I knew exactly what he was capable of, he had shown me that. He got to a point where he didn't have to tell me; my body remembered the physicality, the brutality of what he had done to me.

It wasn't the threat of a maybe, it was the threat it would happen again, and again, and again until I understood that it would keep happening. As if compliance would somehow allow my freedom to be bought with good behaviour. That one day I'd be allowed my freedom if I just behaved and did what he wanted in the meantime.

I struggled to do anything he told me to do.

I tried.

I really fucking tried to do what he wanted.

It just wasn't in me.

It was a pantomime, a dangerous one and I wasn't a good enough actress. I was exactly the best and worst person for him to pick for his victim. My facial expressions are too raw, too difficult to hide. I'd laugh at the wrong moments and never pick up his subtext or implications, or I would be too late.

I was always acting wrong, he'd rely on me to agree with him and continue in his lack of honesty, the stories he'd tell, and I'd have no idea what he was talking about. I think deep down he thought I was like him and was disappointed when I didn't respond in a way he wanted me to.

My childhood abuse turned me into the perfect victim, quick to apologise and never trusting others to tell them the truth in what happens behind closed doors. His childhood abuse made him into someone that would rather abuse than ever allow them to be in a vulnerable position to be abused again. Allan saw me as being weak & vulnerable. By his abuse, he ruined any chances of me having a normal, happy life.

Except it was difficult, so hard not to have my freedom, my ability to make my own choices, my own mistakes. I couldn't keep living like that. Saying that I pushed him? That I provoked him? Except is it really a provocation? Does he really have the right to use physical and sexual violence as a justification of reacting to me saying I wanted to leave?

Pets

When I was sixteen, I got myself a kitten. It was a girl, a Tortoiseshell; mainly black with lots of little orange and white bits everywhere. I named her Miss Daisy Doodles, Doodles for short. I got her from some random person in a flat across town and I carried my kitten, this tiny bag of bones who I would soon discover was riddled in fleas, home where she would stay. I lived with my mother at this time, and she didn't approve but I didn't give a fuck, I wanted a cat, and I was bored and lonely, having just left school and about to start college. I feared my future but was excited too.

When Allan started to come around a few years later when we began dating it was a running joke that Doodles hated him. She attacked him; hissing and making lots of crying and screaming noises towards him. She would chase him, running and jumping towards him. She would hide on top of wardrobes or other high places because he was 5ft11 and she liked to be up somewhere higher than him. Now, looking back this was a red flag because he never did anything to her (that I saw but now I'm not sure - I didn't think he was capable of these things whereas now, nothing would surprise me) but she hated him passionately.

In the end when I moved out of my mum's, I had desperately wanted to take my cat with me and between Allan and my mum, somehow and I can't now remember how the hell they managed this because I loved that cat more than anything. Certainly, more than him. They convinced me to leave the cat behind and that my mum would look after her. I hated them both for it, but I did agree and left. Again, this is how strong manipulation is.

I was sad at having to leave my cat behind, Allan made it his mission to get us a kitten together. This was surprising because he was a stickler for rules (when it suited him) and yet he was willing to go against the landlord's instructions of no animals.

He ended up getting a kitten from someone we both used to work with at Blockbuster, Natalie, who died shortly after this. He was pretty broken up about it and I never figured out why he had such a strong reaction except I now believe that there was something going on between them.

I didn't think that at the time because he was so adamant and believable about not cheating and so aggressive about believing I was cheating on him, when I wasn't. How he hated cheating and cheaters... I didn't put together the information until afterwards. He did tell me that his friend, Marcus had cheated on his wife Jessie with Natalie in the blockbuster store one time, having sex through the back of the shop. I was shocked at hearing this about Marcus but then again, he was friends with Allan and now I think the whole lot of them are just disgusting pigs. I never said anything. It wasn't until later when I was reading and researching more about people like Allan, how they will usually tell stories about their "friends" doing things when it's actually them that's done it.

That they want to talk about these things they've done, usually extremely bad things, but don't want to get in trouble for it so they blame a friend. Let's face it, I was never going to go up to Marcus and asked if he fucked Natalie in the back of the store when they were on shift together. I wasn't interested in other people's lives when mine was always falling apart. I had my hands full.

It does make me wonder about a lot of things he told me. I believed he was telling the truth and yet, I can't verify most of it. It just makes me wonder what the truth really is because it appears to be a lot darker than I even knew at the time or could imagine now.

Anyway, he brought the kitten home, and we had this cat named Jewel, a fully black kitty who was wonderful. A year later, heavily pregnant with my daughter, I had the cat given away because she had kittens' days before I was due to give birth and I was unable to look after them and her knowing the baby was due.

Allan went off his head at me for it, hated me for making him get rid of his cat when animals are for life. He was so strict on everything being "for life." He didn't give up or give in on anything. He was ridiculously stubborn, but I pushed and spoke to his gran and made them give up the cat because I knew I would not be able to care for the cat especially with the kittens. Everyone kept telling me that a baby is easy, that it wasn't going to be as difficult as I made it out to be, that an animal is easy to look after too.

I knew I was going to struggle, Allan had been physically abusive and verbally so angry all the time now at this point. I felt alone and I didn't want to add to my struggles; I wanted life to be as easy as possible and reduce stress not add to it. I can't believe how much I have been villainized for this, but this has been a theme in my life that I will stubbornly cling onto because life is difficult enough without making it worse for yourself or anyone else.

Also, having a baby is the most difficult thing I have ever done. Children are not easy to look after or raise. Anyone who tells you otherwise is full of shit.

Animals and rehoming them is always something that I have been met with anger and disgust which amuses me because would you rather the animal was neglected? That is the reality that I was dealing with. Allan always wanted pets so that he could sit with them and cuddle them. He wanted to take pictures and show off. I think he liked the attention people would give him with a new animal. I was constantly battling with him and telling him no because he wanted every manner of animal;

Piglet, kitten, puppy, ferrets, mice, rabbits, monkey, turtle, tortoise, snakes… Anything that could be a pet he wanted. There were even times when he was driving and if we were on country roads and if he saw sheep out of their pens, he would try and get the sheep into the car to take it home.

Now, a lot of people reading this might think, aww, that's exactly the kind of husband I'd like! That's adorable and yes, that's fine… For you, not for me. I didn't want that and that was a big incompatibility between us, it wasn't something I was willing to compromise on. This was a man who beat me, raped me, screamed at me for merely breathing in the same room as him and this trick with the animals was just another branch of weaponised incompetence, animal cruelty and manipulation.

Here is the list of all the animals that we had during our relationship;

Jewel, cat 2006

Popcorn, dog, 2010

Stripes, cat 2010

Bee, cat 2010

Twinkle, dog, 2012

Cookie, dog, 2013

Mittens, cat, 2013

Snow, dog 2014

Gracie, dog 2014

Grace, dog 2014

Pumpkin, dog 2014

Jasper, cat, 2014

Luke, dog 2015

Lady, dog 2017

Pixie, dog 2019

I also have a few pictures of another black cat/kitten when the kids were both toddler age and I have no idea what that cat's name was or what happened to it.

By the date of his arrest, we had; Twinkle, Cookie, Pixie, Lady and Mittens. Every other animal was given away or rehomed and I was glad for it. That was a hard battle, and he did it begrudgingly. It was also with promises that he would not under any circumstances get another animal.

He always went and got another animal.

There was a kitten that Allan once hid in the downstairs bedroom for two days and didn't tell me until I did find it because he knew I would freak out.

It was a running fucking joke that we always had new animals, and I was embarrassed having to tell anyone at work or my mum about said animals because I never wanted or agreed to them.

My day-to-day life was hard; I hated having to deal with pets on top of it. I'm sorry if that makes you feel any kind of way, I'm not sorry at all, I don't owe anyone an explanation. I was tired all the time. Not just the average way a parent is tired when they have two children, but I was tired from the psychological warfare of dealing with Allan who was more volatile and destructive than any child or pet. One of the dogs once ate through the couch he used to rape me on and I feel that was a good thing, being able to get rid of the ridiculously expensive leather couch that I hated the sight of.

However, the animals were not cared for properly. He would pay for the pet initially, usually through Gumtree paying hundreds for the animal that apparently, we didn't have. He would then manipulate and bully someone to drive him there and back to collect the animal. Now, sometimes this would be across the country. He didn't care; he would always make someone do it for him.

He would do the first vet check-ups for the animal, getting their first jags and flea treatment and then rarely take them back to the vet again. That caused an issue with one of the dogs. I do believe that dog would have lived longer if he had been regularly taken in for routine checkups and would have picked up on the health condition he had sooner and leading to him being treated for it. More on that story later though.

He would not pay for vets; he would not pay for anything the animal needed. He would sit and cuddle it. He would only buy the cheapest food and cat litter possible. He wouldn't brush them, bathe them or play with them. He never walked them unless it was done under me losing my fucking temper and he would take a dog for a walk but that was lucky if it happened once every six months.

The animals would in boredom and lack of training destroy the house. The number of times we were all covered in flea bites and throwing out bedding, bean bags, rugs and dog beds to try and get rid of fleas was disgusting and I hated him for it. Fleas were a recurring issue FOR YEARS. I could never get on top of cleaning enough for the four bedrooms, three level townhouse that we lived in to stop the flea problem. It drove me fucking mad.

The kids lost so many toys and things from their rooms either because of animals doing the toilet in the house or from the constant infestation of fleas we always had because of whatever new animal he had brought into the house.

Now, if you want to live like that, that's your choice… You can do whatever you want in your own house but not me, I cannot live like that. I didn't want to.

He would use the animals and the kids to manipulate me, he would tell the kids he was getting the animal first and they would excitably tell me about the new puppy we were getting. I'd be forced to go along because otherwise, I'd be the one disappointing the kids and he would do it anyway regardless of what I said. He would cause me to upset the kids for nothing.

I just wanted a sensible man for a partner, someone who cared about our home and our life together. He only wanted to hurt me, break me down, wear me out and abuse me. He did these things to hurt me. That was his intention. He would laugh at me for any reactions I had.

Every time I came home, I was coming home to shit and piss on the floor somewhere. I would be standing in it, sliding in it, falling in it. So, would the kids. We'd be ready to go out to school or off on a trip with him, and someone would end up with shit on them and I'd have to get the child stripped and changed.

I was the one cleaning everything, all the time and this was made worse by the animals. The house smelled bad, and we probably did too. There were animals who would pee on top of clean washing piles and in baskets, like toy baskets. I was constantly fed up, angry and shouting at the never-ending mess and he thought it was funny. He never helped. He would just laugh at me or get annoyed at me being annoyed.

THE BEGINNING OF THE END

At this time, I didn't know that the end was in sight. Or an end at least.

I remember one time with friends he laughed and joked about how bad I was in bed. How I was a "sack of potatoes" and just lay there.

The thing is, even if he was trying to insult me, it's not something I've ever cared about, I know I'm not bad in bed, that's subjective. It comes from practice and having a safe environment to do so in.

If he was trying to put other men off trying to steal me from him, then again, it never worked because any one of his friends would have taken me off his hands with minimal fuss. They are all a gang of assholes.

However, the funny thing about men and rape that they don't seem to realise is that if you are raping someone, if you are forcing them to do so then lying there, like a sack of potatoes is exactly what they are going to do. If you rape me, your pleasure during that rape, is not my concern. I am not going to do a damn thing to make it more pleasurable for you.

He used to ask me to "make noises" for him. The interesting thing about me is I am incapable of faking an orgasm. Or faking enjoyment at all.

When he was raping me, he would do everything it seemed to convince me or himself that it wasn't rape, that it was consensual. Sometimes he's come out with truly horrible things that made me realise he knew exactly what he was doing.

"You're so wet, do you feel how wet you are?" This was his defence of how that it might have started off as rape, my body was obviously enjoying it. This made him feel like I was being deliberately unfair to him by saying no, that I would enjoy it if I gave it a chance. This let him off the hook because he "got me wet." What he failed to realise about this was that happens sometimes. The body reacts, doesn't mean it's consensual. The consent part has nothing to do with how a body reacts and everything to do with the person and what they want and choose for themselves.

Also, the "wetness" he was feeling wasn't always vaginal lubrication. Mostly it was urine because I had wet myself in fright or most likely because that's a common occurrence when you've been strangled. Your bladder loosens. There were times it was also blood.

"Make some noise and it'll be over faster." This angered me so much when he'd say this, struggling to hold an erection while he was raping me, struggling to stay hard as I cried or hit him, kicked him, scratched at him to get off me. He wanted me to pretend to moan and enjoy myself, give him the illusion that I was enjoying it, enjoying him. I can only imagine how I looked at him then, utterly silent in my defiance.

"Stop crying, I'll go soft."

The blatant contradictions in how he abused me confused me so much. It was also something later that was used against me in court because everything contradicted itself in his behaviour and nothing made any sense. Sometimes I was positive he was truly sadistic, and it was the fighting, the violence, that turned him on and got him off. Sometimes he genuinely seemed to want to have consensual sex with me, wanting me to enjoy it.

If I wasn't actively trying to fight him off, I would lie there and stare at him. I would make constant eye contact and make sure I blinked as little as possible so he could see the anger and hatred I felt towards him. If that was the only defiance I had in me, I did it. I would verbally tell him while he was raping me that he was raping me.

If all I could do was stare him out, then that is what I did. If he let me use my legs or arms, I would have continued hitting and kicking him until I had pissed him off enough to stop… Which I don't think ever actually happened, he always found some way to threaten me into something of a submission. I still stared angrily and held eye contact. I never let him away with it, I rebelled as much as I could, and I am saner for it.

It's the few times that I froze and was unable to react that haunt me. And it shouldn't because my body and brain did whatever it had to, to survive.

Then, to me, there was the most effective and worst thing he would say to me to force my compliance, "If you don't let me, I'll shout the kids in and rape you in front of them." What was I supposed to do? The terror I felt at them being made to watch something like that. All I could do was try and endure and I hated him for it.

***

When he was unemployed (and yes, I know, this was the worst idea regarding him being a stay-at-home dad because honestly, he was a master of weaponising incompetence) he oversaw the house, the pets and the kids. This happened because he had moved to a job he had wanted but ended up not being good enough for. During his probation period it was made clear, he was unlikely to be kept on. Since my job was safe and secure, he ended his employment before they had a chance to let him go and I remained at work.

So, what would he do? Sit on his arse and masturbate. He told me he would masturbate up to eight times a day. Which is hilarious when we get to a later segment of the series and part of his defence in court being that he had erectile dysfunction. I wish I had been quicker and wittier at the time to state that the boxers, socks and T-shirts covered in come daily would suggest otherwise but I was so shocked I didn't. That's a story for later though.

Also, if he genuinely had erectile dysfunction and didn't hit me or rape me, I might have stayed. I didn't want to break up our family, I didn't want to take my kids away from their father.

He would go and collect my mum, pick her up and take her to mine so she could take care of the animals & clean the house then deposit her back home afterwards. He would then get the kids from school. Sometimes he even came and picked me up from work!

For someone who rarely did pick me up at home time, he did usually spend lunch time with me. Again, you might think, aww that's cute, he missed her. That's what his constant texts or emails would say but he was both codependent on me and didn't like me having a chance to interact with others. What would happen to him if I made friends with anyone? What if I cheated on him?

Mostly at work I sat on my own downstairs away from the main eating area and played Pokémon Go because my workplace was a gym. Yes, I am that kind of nerd. I needed the silence and time to decompress because the workplace itself was loud and busy, and I didn't get much time to relax and destress.

Of course, I never got that at home. So, he would make me sandwiches (I know, another nice gesture proving he could when he wanted to. Or he would take me to buy something, Pizza Hut used to be right next to my workplace) I'd sit with him until my lunch hour was up. Then I'd have a busy afternoon and go home to the fucking mess he managed to make in the tiny amount of time when my mum had gone home (yes, he did leave her at the house while he fucked off out, he did this regularly she later told me. She had also been told not to tell me she had even been at the house).

I don't know how one person managed to make as much mess as he did.

This is a man who pissed I'm positive from the door of the bathroom, towards the general direction of the toilet if the mess was to be understood. You would walk into the bathroom and the whole floor, wall and toilet itself, not only the seat, but everything was covered in pee. He blamed the kids; it wasn't the kids. There was a literal puddle of urine multiple times a day.

His personal hygiene was gross and got worse over time. Again, I understand that his weight and his mental health had a negative impact on this BUT it was long term, and he never sought help. He told me he would see the GP, he either didn't, or he'd lie about it.

This is a man who didn't believe in wiping his bum when he did a shit or washing his hands and yet he wondered why I didn't want him touching me with those hands? Why did I refuse him putting his fingers inside me? Why would I want that? Rape trauma aside, that's disgusting.

His arse was thick with shit, he smelled bad. His underwear always had a streak up the back from where it contacted his skin. He would walk around in nothing but his boxer shorts so these would stain through to the couch and bed. Then when he was naked, which was also a lot, he would sit with his shitty arse directly on the couch or bed. I would wake up in the morning and the stink of shit would make me gag. There would always be streaks of shit on the bed covers AND the couch.

I would have to strip the bed and wash it every day.

I would have to scrub the couch every day

I'd end up throwing out cushions because they stank of his shit and his sweaty testicles. I had one of his friends smell a cushion, give it to me telling me it stank of sweaty balls as if it was me who had caused the smell.

While he was unemployed, he was raping me once a day at least. I say at least because sometimes it was just at night, sometimes it was more than once a night. Sometimes it would also happen in the morning. Most mornings he raped me, I'd be in such a depressive mood, also from the pain and lack of sleep, that he would take me to McDonalds and buy me a breakfast meal. I'd laugh walking into work, delirious with depression holding my large coke drink knowing that it was a sign of what had happened to me, and no one knew.

They could maybe see it in me, see it in my eyes, pretty sure the light left them a long time ago.

Recently I had been going through photographs from when I was eighteen to the last few days and was shocked by how dead my eyes are and have been all these years. There is no fucking light in them at all. There's a brief period in 2020/2021 where my eyes have a little sparkle, it's almost like it was coming back… Until someone else drove the final nails into my coffin.

***

I remember his friends sitting at the table and Allan coming out with something else awful about me. I can't even remember what now, it was always something, something about me being bad in bed, or a whore who was fucking anyone, or a slut or a crazy psycho bitch and I remember Irvine laughing, "I'm just waiting for the day we all get the phone call that Lou needs help hiding your body!"

They all laughed like assholes do and I stayed silent. Absolutely meaning it when I stared at him to respond, "You'd never get that call because I wouldn't trust a single one of you." Turning to Allan to finish, "Besides, I wouldn't need any help to hide a body."

Allan nodded, I knew that look, he was almost impressed, as much as he can be with someone he barely viewed as a person. He knew he was on thin ice with me, my mental health not capable of holding together much longer without absolutely snapping. This was the point where I believe I was on the verge of a complete psychotic break. I was convinced that he was going to push me to murder him, or that he would murder me or that I would kill myself.

I was positive that one of us dying was the only way out of this marriage.

Irvine never really replied, the conversation changed, and no doubt was just another perfect example of how crazy and unhinged I was. How no one would believe I was in any danger and if anyone was, perhaps it was Allan.

How to tell people that he was constantly pushing all my buttons. He was a perfect master of the marionette, always pulling on my strings and getting exactly the reaction he was looking for.

Me? I just reacted; I refused to be bullied so I tried to stand up for myself. I refused to be hit, so I tried to stand up for myself and fight back. I refused to be raped so I tried to stop him using any method or means I could. He always overpowered me though, the truth being that most of the time he probably was holding back, allowing me to fight him because I genuinely believe now, that the fighting is what got him off. That's what really turned him on.

I don't like how you get condemned for fighting back and yet you also get condemned if you don't. What was I supposed to do?

What I do know is that during that length of time, what helped my mental health the most was knowing that I tried to fight him off. I never made it easy and that even as delusional as he was, he could not mistake my actions for compliance or consent. He knew, he knew exactly what he was doing every minute he was doing it.

I do believe that my mental health only survived because I mostly always fought back.

THE LAST HOUSE

NOVEMBER 2017 – JULY 2019

She's a crazy, psycho bitch

I once had an argument with Sarah where she had said psychological abuse was worse than physical or sexual abuse from a partner.

I said that for all the abuse I had suffered, my husband sitting at the head of the table and saying it anyway, that rape has always been worse for me.

How did no one sitting there put two and two together and realise that I was talking about the man I was married to and not some obscure boyfriend from the past when I had in fact, never really dated anyone properly prior to him?

I can see her point, I can see anyone's point when they talk about their experiences of abuse because ultimately anyone's experience of abuse is personal. They are entitled to feel however they feel. Their emotions and feelings should be believed and validated as they are. Your opinion and mine are not required.

At the time, I was battling against myself, constantly trying to stay afloat when I felt like I was visibility drowning in front of everyone who was there that evening. My so-called friends.

Now, I know that abuse of any kind causes trauma in the body and in the brain. That trauma is personal to the individual and varies from person to person by severity. No one's experience should be minimised and this competition that people seem to have with one another about one person's trauma being worse than someone else's is pointless and wrong. Not just academically incorrect but also it suggests that your trauma isn't as important as someone else's because there will always be someone who "has had it worse." Again, that's not how it works. Abuse of any type is astronomically devastating and damaging to the person experiencing it.

To me, being raped was and is the worst trauma I've ever experienced. To her, the psychological aspect was worse. Both are right and both are valid.

But worse is subjective too, because the damage that the psychological trauma which was done to me has never left me. It's because of that trauma that I went from being in an abusive marriage with Allan, to two and a half years later after a forced healing journey that I ended up in another abusive situation with someone else. I genuinely thought, that will never happen to me again and guess what? It happened to me again. I can't even call that an actual relationship since it turned out I was being used by that person to cheat on an actual partner.

That's a story for another time.

However, it is only from trying to date afterwards that I learned some of the tricks Allan had used on me for what they were. That some things he told me were lies and how some sexual things with him that I thought were normal, were in fact, not normal at all. This man was sadistic. He used my lack of experience in dating and sex to abuse me further. He also made me more vulnerable afterwards to being taken advantage of and abused by others.

I've had enough

Eventually I sat him down and said categorically that I had no memory of what he had accused me of on the night of his birthday party in 2010. That seven years later, coming up on eight I was fed up of having to defend myself. I was pissed off that he was using this as an excuse to beat me.

Not for the first time, I told him I'd had enough. I did not know what had happened, but I was refusing to move forward even one more day of him holding it over my head. He had spent seven years punching me, slapping me, pulling my hair, strangling me, raping me anally, vaginally and orally because he believed I'd had sex with Blake, despite the fact I was black out, unconscious drunk and had no memory of anything after a certain point that night.

Allan is the last thing I remember of that night.

I told him that I was accepting that it had happened, that I didn't remember but for the sake of moving forward I was taking the blame. So, he had two choices; either forgive me for it and move on, never using it to harm me again OR if he couldn't forgive me, which I accepted as a possibility, then we should separate.

He refused to acknowledge me or the conversation, getting up and leaving me sitting in the kitchen by myself. Everything carried on the same as it ever was.

The Best Friend and My Biggest Source of Shame

Blake.

Here is one of my biggest confessions and as I only recently realised; the reason I believed that I deserved the abuse. In the last few years, the reason I kept myself small and believed I was a bad person, that I deserved harm over real love. I dated men beneath me, not thinking I deserved better.

Blake.

It all started in the first month I had been dating Allan, and he introduced me to someone he had gone on at length about; his best friend Blake. They had met before they started school when Blake's parents had separated, his mother moving into a house a few doors down from Allan's gran. They were instant friends and as such, it was important for us to be introduced.

He had been living in Glasgow with his girlfriend Natalie, they were supposed to meet up at Christmas; to introduce me but Allan had put that off considering what had happened to me just days before that

Christmas. Unknown to me at the time, Allan had told Blake he was already dating me and had been for months at that point.

The first thing he said to me was, "I remember you from primary school." I never got a chance to ask what he meant. Allan was my boyfriend, and I was happy at the time, it was all so new so looking at his ridiculously attractive best friend did little for me in the sense of thinking of Blake at the time. He was stunning. He was 21 then, I was still 19. Did I fall in love with him then? Truthfully, I don't remember.

I've told myself over the years that my "crush" on Blake was one-sided and started much later, once the abuse from Allan was well established but I was obsessed with Blake right from the beginning. That's the effect he had on everyone, it wasn't just me.

Have you ever met someone and instantly gotten along with them? A Leo to my Aries, he was instantly my friend too; we'd laugh over anything, nothing but giggling and bullying one another. We were loud and stupid; we had a great time together even if all we were doing was talking.

I can only imagine how embarrassing the way we were around one another was to his girlfriend and my husband. I chased after him like a puppy. I'm not going to downplay it; it was disrespectful to Allan. It was mutual though.

Blake was the type who hugged me the moment he saw me and held on way too long, it was never enough. Allan got angry at this, never bringing it up with Blake himself, instead making me tell him not to touch me anymore. I can still remember the hurt on his face while we stood in my kitchen having that conversation. He reluctantly agreed.

Another man who felt entitled to my body and probably wouldn't have respected the word no.

When he held his arms open to me years later, I went into them not caring that Allan was standing watching. I was broken at this time and desperately needed to be held. No one has ever held me the way Blake did. A feeling I'd long be chasing after in all the wrong people. I remember him saying softly to me, "So you're finally hugging me back then?" And I can still hear the bitterness in his tone at me rejecting him all those years. Did no one understand that it wasn't my choice? Allan would literally beat me for smiling at Blake, at any man. Convinced I'd run off with anyone.

Allan had reason to worry. If Blake had said, "Lou, I'm taking you and the kids with me." I'd never have wasted time packing a bag.

I remember dancing with him at my wedding. He was the best man and the third person I danced with. Hugely pregnant, I was struggling but I enjoyed dancing with him. Or me, moving as best I could. Even at the wedding all I could think was, I should be marrying you. Or not marrying at all and going off, being young and enjoying life.

We talked about moving to Australia, being at the beach as often as possible, and always being in the sun. With our respective partners, of course.

It was Blake who casually brought up how hot I was naked and I asked how he would know such a thing. He mentioned the nudes of mine Allan had shown him back when we had first started dating, pictures I had shared privately. He was mortified to know Allan had shared those with him without my permission.

I have a picture Allan took of us in TGI Friday's me smiling drunkenly at the camera, Blake drinking his cocktail through a straw, but his face is turned to me, staring, smiling in adoration. You can see how he feels about me in his eyes.

There was a moment on my tenth wedding anniversary, I hadn't seen Blake in a year or two at this point, he turned towards me and mid-sentence went speechless at the sight of me done up in a pretty dress. That was normal in the beginning for me, but the more time went on and the more depressed I became, this was unusual. I barely wore makeup at that time, and rarely did my hair. He made me feel beautiful, not with anything he said because he always complimented me, but it was in his silence, the stunned lack of speech and the look on his face as he saw me. I felt like the most beautiful woman in the world, I felt seen.

At a time when I hated myself, was overweight and struggling with everything from my hair to my waistline, he made me feel good about myself. I could have bottled that feeling, something I've lacked almost exclusively before and since.

It didn't matter if I was pregnant, skinny, slim, overweight. It never mattered what length my hair was or what I wore, he always made me feel beautiful.

Holding me, his hugs, his hands on me, the protective stance he would take made me feel feminine and safe. No one has ever made me feel like that, Allan never did, and no one has since.

I remember that night, we stood at the bar, and he bought me a drink, telling everyone I was his best friend to which I said, obviously but you're not mine. I watched his face drop as I explained that he was maybe my second or third best friend. I told him he had abandoned me, that he didn't come around much anymore. We both knew he had distanced himself from Allan after whatever happened the night of Allan's birthday all the way back in 2010. I missed him, I told him that.

From Allan's point of view, this must have pissed him off massively. I get it, for years I believed it was the reason he beat me as badly as he did. The anger he felt towards me and how bad a person I was for it, I deserved it all.

When the police got involved, I told them that I understood why Allan hit me, but he should have left me rather than stay with me. The DC asked me to explain what had happened that night. I did, I explained how I was drunk, got more drunk, was black out unconscious and according to Allan, he had walked in on Blake & I had sex in the downstairs bedroom of our house. At his birthday party.

I explained this and felt satisfied at being honest about it, shamed and full of self-loathing that I had done that at all. I had thought about it but there is a difference between thinking about something and doing it. I didn't like that I was that kind of person. I liked to think of myself as honest, trustworthy.

The DC looked at me with nothing but concern & pity asking if I also wanted to press rape charges against Blake.

RAPE?

Blake?

I fucking froze. I had spent years with Allan telling me that I had cheated on him that night. First, he told me that he had seen me kissing Blake. That he had overheard Natalie screaming at Blake, "That's your best friend's wife."

He had once told me that he had instead seen me kissing Ryan (Yes, Ryan the Rapist) and I recoiled violently at that one. He never brought up Ryan in that context ever again. It makes me wonder what the fuck happened that night.

He told me that the reason he first punched me in July 2010, was because the anger over me kissing Blake and cheating on him was too much and he had lost control that day finally after bottling it up for those couple of months.

After the violence ramped up in August 2016, I had no explanation as to why. Now I do believe something sinister happened to cause him to act the way he did that month. He blamed me, but I don't think that's accurate, I think he's using that as a cover. I had pressed him for answers about why he had suddenly changed, and the violence had gotten worse.

On January 2nd, 2017, he told me, and my depression took a hit, and my brain never really recovered from this moment. He told me that it wasn't just a kiss that he had walked in and seen me having sex with Blake.

I fucking hated myself as a result.

I believed him without question. How could I ask for more information? I would only upset him. I wanted to speak to Blake, but they had drifted further apart over the years. It became very awkward.

I remember one night I had tried to speak to Blake about it. I was too scared to ask. We drunkenly stumbled up the street from the pub to the cinema, arms around one another trying not to fall over. "We shouldn't be alone together," is what he had said to me. I wanted to ask why but I couldn't say the words out loud.

Allan blamed me for that too. That I had fucked up his friendship with the one person who I knew he cared about. Maybe the only person Allan cared about.

Over the years it was part of the psychological games he played with me. Always asking, always wanting to know what I remembered of that night. I told him every single time the same story and it's never changed. I have no memory of what happened after a certain point that night. I remember playing Just Dance with Ryan on the Wii in the living room. I turned away from Ryan, I saw Michael, Blake, Natalie and Allan in the kitchen and staggering I walked towards them. It's fuzzy and I don't remember making it to the kitchen.

I woke up in my bed covered in vomit. It was in my hair, on me and all over the bedsheets and the floor. I thought maybe I had been sick during the night and fallen back asleep. I was only wearing my t-shirt from the night before. I had no bra or pants on, not even socks. I just had a terrible feeling that something bad had happened to me.

One thing I do know is that my vagina was bare but clean. Allan had a habit of ejaculating inside of me and never felt any need to clean me up or assist in any way. The fact I was free of come, made me wonder seriously about what had happened. I have my theories, and they are all awful. I wonder if he not only plied me with alcohol but drugged me, would not have been the first time. I wonder about a lot of different things.

I told him the same thing repeatedly, he was never satisfied but again, I wonder if he was just making sure I hadn't remembered anything that might condemn him.

He used Blake as an excuse for every time he got angry, every time I asked him to do something. It was constant, he never let up and never let it go.

It was also a direct contradiction because he believed I had cheated on him and yet, he had said repeatedly over the years that if I cheated on him, he'd leave me in a heartbeat because he would be so disgusted by me he wouldn't be able to look at me. I had considered cheating for this reason alone but always held back because I felt he was lying, using it to trap me into doing something I didn't want to do just so he could use it as another excuse to harm me.

I remember a few conversations where he seemed to be actively trying to turn me off Blake, once saying that I would never cope being with Blake because of the attention he gets when out from other women, that I would be too jealous. Another time he told me that he had seen Blake naked lots of times and that I would be disappointed because Blake's penis was smaller than his. As if that mattered to me. He actively told me I wasn't good enough for Blake, that his friend deserved better than me.

Did he mean himself?

Honestly, no one deserved Allan as a romantic interest, I don't hate anyone enough to wish that on them.

It felt odd to me, how hard he tried to put a wedge between us and yet we were always magnetically drawn to one another.

Blake was like sunshine, and I was a sunflower drawn to his radiance. A lot of people like to take someone who shines so brightly and steal it away for themselves, use that light. Yet I only ever wanted to support him to shine brighter. We always brought out the best in each other. I adored him fully. It wasn't just because he was hot, he was but he was so much fun to be around.

Over time I watched panicking as that light started to go out. By the end of my relationship with Allan I was genuinely worried about Blake. Was it guilt?

No one was that worried about me however and certainty no one has reached out to me to check and see if I was ok. It took almost a year for it to sink in what the DC had told me, explained about consent and alcohol and intent.

It took a whole year, taking me into the summer of 2020 to realise that my daydreams and fantasies about ending up with Blake were unrealistic and potentially dangerous. That he would never leave his best friend for me. Afterall, who we choose as our friends is a direct reflection of who we are ourselves. If that was his best friend then what I saw in Blake was most likely just a false charm, right? He was the light to Allan's darkness, but really aren't they both just the same? Was Blake a victim of Allan's, like I was? Or complicit and involved?

I have no idea, and I've never risked my safety to find out.

I won't.

I said no to the DC, telling her that no matter how drunk I was, anything that happened with Blake would have been consensual, that I would have wanted it to happen. It was the consequence of my own actions. I fucked around and found out. I was still struggling with understanding consent, and what I was entitled to myself. I couldn't wrap my head around Blake taking advantage of me. Not when I had all but thrown myself at him that night. I had literally chased him around the house, mainly so I could wear his medal he had won doing MMA.

It's the person's intent that matters, what did they mean to do. If he chose to wait and take advantage of me when I was drunk or drugged, then it is rape.

I told the DC though that I had no memory and I knew that Allan was a liar. Of course it would be just like him, getting the last laugh, driving a wedge between us to make sure we'd never be together. A ticking time bomb he knew would eventually go off on me. Allan might have lied about the whole thing, and I refused to falsely accuse someone of rape.

Then the chill started, it was a terror I'd never known as I thought about how Allan would react if Blake was arrested for raping me. Getting Allan arrested was already an offence of highest treason to my now ex-husband, the worst thing I could ever do to him. But Blake, I knew that would be the final nail in my coffin, I'd never have lived to the end of the week if Blake had been arrested for rape because of me.

My psychiatrist

I was given a diagnosis of bipolar mixed affective disorder in January 2018, and I almost gave up at the news. It felt wrong somehow that I was the one with a serious mental health condition when he literally rapes me for fun.

What followed was a year and a half of psychiatric appointments, trying nearly every single medication known for the disorder. None of them worked (I wonder why? Perhaps because I never had bipolar disorder to begin with and in fact was neurodivergent, extremely depressed, burnt out and suffering from huge amounts of trauma). The medications were mostly antipsychotics, some anti-convulsants and all had massively detrimental impacts to my physical and mental health.

As soon as my diagnosis was confirmed Allan went out of his way to tell EVERYONE about it. He called and texted every single family member, friend and even sat down with our two children and explained it to them.

He had what he wanted, I was now officially labelled as mentally unstable by a psychiatrist and actively taking medication for said disorder.

I remember being in Asda with him one day. We bumped into someone we hadn't seen from our previous job in years, and he spoke to them, told them about it. Most people catch up about holidays, or new babies, promotions but not Allan. He made sure to tell everyone his wife was mentally ill, had not just regular bipolar but I was special and had mixed affective bipolar disorder. "Doesn't that make so much sense?" He'd ask, and they'd nod and agree.

He would do this in front of me, so God only knows what he was saying about me behind my back.

I was fucked.

One incident that still unsettles me now was one evening as I was going to bed and he took advantage of me under the influence of one of the medications. I can't remember which one it was, I was on so many at that time. A side effect was that as soon as I took the tablet, I was literally knocked out cold within 10 minutes. This, for me who had suffered constantly with insomnia and never felt like I got a decent night's sleep was, to begin with, a great thing.

Since I had a strict routine, I had to follow at night, I made sure to do everything and only take my medication once I was sure all my chores were done. I'd take the tablet when I was in bed, knowing the effect it would have on me. One night, I forgot about something in the kitchen and went running through. I had already taken the tablet. I made it back to my bedroom, but as I stood at the end of the bed, I felt woozy. My legs started going from under me and I remember saying, "It's starting…"

I remember him pushing me onto the bed, making sure I was on my back. I could feel him grabbing my legs as he would normally, pulling me down towards the edge where he now stood. "Don't worry…" Was what he said as I felt him pulling off my Pj trousers and pants.

It's these kinds of incidents where someone has said to me, maybe it's best not to remember. My imagination is far too great for that. I'd rather know because perhaps what happened is worse than I could think of, perhaps not. I like to know the truth. The fact is, he liked me unconscious because he liked me not fighting back. Lately I've begun to think his sexual appetite is a lot more sickening than even that.

What I do know is that in the morning after realising what he had done, how vulnerable the medication made me at night. I made an emergency appointment with my psychiatrist and never took that medication again. It also for years would leave me paranoid about taking any medication at all for any reason.

Attempted Drowning

He sat with the lid of the toilet down, probably the only time he ever put the seat or lid down at all and sat leaning forward, his elbows being held up by his knees, his face covered by those massive hands.

Lying in the bath like this was far more vulnerable than I liked. I hated the way my body had twisted and changed, expanded and swollen in all the wrong places. I had curves I didn't want, had never wanted.

I was never happy when I looked like that. A body only made through extreme starvation and over exercise. Something I didn't have the energy for anymore. Food had become a comfort, something that made me feel a little better in the moment while I was eating. It had become an addiction, a feeling so rare I chased it. It was a bitter cycle, destined to repeat, leaving me feeling more frustrated and unhappy than ever.

There were some benefits to letting myself go, I believed that his friends would no longer find me attractive if I were overweight and therefore would stop making these horrible comments about me. I didn't do this for me exactly; I did it for Allan so that he wouldn't have to listen to his friends talk about me that way. Maybe then he'd realise no one wanted me and I wasn't cheating on him.

I also liked the extra weight because contrary to my outdated beliefs, being overweight may have made physical activity more difficult but it had given me the weight and strength to not allow him to throw me around as easily as he once had. I was able to put up more of a fight. I was able to hold my ground a little better. It made me feel a little safer. I had also hoped that since he had called me fat as an insult so many times in the past that he would no longer be attracted to me and leave me for someone else. That's what I hoped for most of all. My daydreams consisted of him telling me he had found someone younger and prettier and was leaving me for her. Oh yes please. How I longed to be discarded and left on my own with the kids. There was nothing else I prayed for more aside from wanting to die of course.

He was also an asshole for ever calling me fat in the first place, knowing that I had been deeply insecure about my weight. Allan had also always been overweight the whole time I'd known him. I had never seen that as a negative regarding him as a person. My issue always was that he complained about it constantly, did nothing about it but expected me to make him magically lose weight somehow. Again, it was my fault he was overweight and unhappy within himself.

The days of being nice to him were long gone, feigning kindness for the sake of appearances. I had started to become as nasty towards him as he had been towards me. It would take me a few years before realising that again, every bad word he said towards me was just a projection of how he felt about himself. No part of me could ever again be sympathetic towards him, regardless of his own inner demons. I had given him a safe place, free of judgement and I would have stood by him through everything if he had kept his hands off me. I would never have rejected him for his own insecurities, no matter how bad they had been. Or at least, at that time, I believed that.

Still, he was the overweight one, not me or at least not at that time. Instead of building up my confidence he had worn me down to hate myself completely, inside and out. I hated my body, hated every lumpy round part. I was disgusted by what I saw so I never looked, not when I was naked, avoided mirrors, I truly believed what he had told me. That I was ugly, unattractive, unwanted and had long lost any appeal.

No one will ever want me.

It was both a point of pain and a relief.

I would realise much later that men would always find me attractive and want to get to know me, want to have sex with me. Men, generally, don't like me because of my personality, not my face or body.

So, already feeling bad about myself, I was self-conscious of him being in the room with me while I was naked. I didn't want to think about all the negative comments he would make about my appearance but couldn't help overthinking about it anyway. What he voiced out loud mirrored the voice in my head that was and always had been too critical of me my whole life. I was nothing if I was not young and beautiful anymore. I had nothing to offer anyone. I did believe that at the time.

He sat there mostly in silence, coughing as he had been most of that year. He refused to get checked out by a doctor because as much of a hypochondriac as he was, he knew there could be something wrong, having a cough like that which wasn't going away. He had never smoked, never smelled anything from him so it was unlikely due to his poor hygiene that he was doing anything sneaky like drugs behind my back.

I was always on edge in his presence, and he had the door mostly closed over which frightened me. I liked having the door wide open, no secrets that way, nothing to hide. I never closed the door even while I was at the toilet. Besides, the steam from the bath would make the room too hot for me, I'd soon feel faint.

I'm not sure what happened next exactly except for when he did something that truly frightened me and was a direct extract from the book of how to destroy my sanity. He stood, crossed to me, kneeled with some effort on the floor next to the bath and placed his hands on my chest. Those giant hands which had caused so much damage to me already. He pushed me down and held me under the water.

It happened so fast I had little time to react or understand what was happening, only that I was scared. The fear was unimaginable and was everything I had expected this to be. My whole life I had feared water. I had never learned to swim, following two incidents when I was around five years old, two separate incidents where I almost drowned. Water was my biggest fear; I had never willingly put my head beneath the bathwater before. I had never submerged my face in water, never even stood fully underneath the shower before as water on my face was a huge issue for me.

I thrashed about wildly trying to get him to release his hands from my chest, digging and clawing at his hands, desperate to move myself away from his grip. His hands were too large, my fear too overwhelming. I couldn't scream, I couldn't breathe, I was positive I was going to die, again.

As quick as it started, it ended. He rose from where he had been kneeling and stood, drying his hands on a towel before glancing at me, recovering. Too scared to get out of the bath but terrified to stay in it. I kicked the plug out and let the bath drain before he could come back again. He left me there without a word and closed the door on his way out.

I lay there, shivering, terrified and alone in the bathroom wondering what the hell had happened. What had I done to deserve that and why the hell had he done that to me? He knew exactly how I felt about water, about having my head underneath and the impact that had on me. It was deliberate, he had deliberately done this to me. He knew and he did it anyway.

Suddenly flashing back to our holiday in Spain all those years prior when he carried me out to the ocean and dumped me in the water, telling me it was the best way to learn how to swim. It failed of course and resulted in me being fucking angry at him.

I didn't have the strength to be angry, I was scared. He had tried to kill me then left as if it was nothing. Was it a warning? I got out of the bath, wrapped myself in a towel and practically ran to the bedroom to get some clothes on before anything else could happen to me.

Unconscious is what he prefers me

After he had attacked me so badly and my mental health (or is it physical health because I do wonder if it's a brain injury I received because the symptoms are so similar to what I've dismissed as merely depression?) deteriorated so much that what started to help was my little delusion about the marriage ending and me finding my soulmate.

Yes, you can laugh at me, I do now too.

At the time, the idea that as a 30-something-year-old with two young children, I would leave this marriage and him behind and meet someone else. This magical someone else was what kept me going. The idea that I could find someone who liked me for me, was attracted to me and who would fall in love with me. It would be real, it would be genuine, and it would be true. This person, this man because I am tragically romantically attracted to men, would show not only me but both kids that not all men are like their father. That there are genuine, real and wonderful men out there. He would be the father the kids never had, he would be the friend, lover and partner that I had never had either. Together, we would build a life and a home together.

That is the fantasy that got me through being beaten, hit, punched, slapped, thrown around, raped vaginally, orally and anally. That is what helped, afterwards, I would think about this faceless man and how he would never hit me, how appalled he would be once I eventually told him about all the things that Allan had done to me. How he would never lay a finger on me without my consent, how he would care about my feelings and my mental health. It felt real, like it was something that could happen. In that fantasy we get married, and we have a baby and he is a wonderful father to his child too.

None of that happened and now I'd never have a child with a man again.

I'd be too scared to get married, and I'd never agree to change my name.

I wouldn't want to live with someone.

The idea of being financially dependent on another person makes me physically sick.

This fantasy, as useless and stupid to me now, was what helped get me through the worst moments in my life. I never wanted to have another child with Allan and yet, he became fixated on getting me pregnant in those last years. Going as far to threaten me with waiting until I was asleep and using a turkey baster to impregnate me with one of his friend's semen. He said they would do that for him. I was terrified.

However, on my limited knowledge at this time, I didn't want to bring another child into this household, I already felt awful for my own two children who deserved a father who loved them and cared about them and every day that passed, every time he hit me or hurt me, I felt that would never be Allan.

I didn't feel another baby would do anything but trap me further, make it more difficult to escape. Two was difficult enough, three would be impossible. I was lucky that he had the vasectomy as I would have already had a few more and probably would have thrown myself off one of the two bridges in the town that were perfect for committing suicide.

I didn't want to look after another child and I was convinced that any baby I'd have would be as mentally ill as me, I couldn't do that. At the time, I didn't feel that he would harm the child exactly, but the living environment was too volatile and not safe. So, he had started looking into reversing his vasectomy, and I just went along because there was absolutely nothing I could do about it.

Soon, after seeing the cost of the reversal by going private he wasn't able to afford it. Looking back, I'm surprised because when I wanted something, there was never any money for it and yet, when he really wanted something no matter the cost, he always found a way.

He fucking confused me, a lot of things did not make sense to me and yet, it would only be with distance and time that little puzzle pieces would come together and form a picture that in the moment, I never even considered. That's another downside to being abused and being in survival mode non-stop is being constantly in the moment. It's hard to see the bigger picture, it's difficult to question things. Unfortunately, all that came later for me and I'm still left with no answers to serious questions such as;

Did he ever have a vasectomy?

There were so many inconsistencies with his stories, his sexual health.

The potential other children he has fathered.

Those two miscarriages I'm convinced I had but have no proof of, how he gaslit me, convinced I must have cheated on him when I hadn't.

How much damage has this man done to my body that I've never even thought to bring up with a doctor because he lied and gaslit me so much?

Even if he did have the vasectomy, it was the constant confusion he caused by being inconsistent that again, made me feel like I was going crazy. That I couldn't trust myself or my own body. The conspiracy theorist, another way to make me seem unstable to others.

"I'lL kIlL mYsElF..."

"If you leave me, I will kill myself."

The statement was one I'd heard before, so many times that any emotional effect that he was looking for was numbed. If I really thought about it, the reality of him killing himself would be a blessing for us. I had fantasied about his death in many ways and what would happen after was the perfect solution. If he died, from suicide, a car crash or natural causes then we would all be free from him. No one would ever have to know what had happened, the kids would be young enough that they would get over his death and be free of his influence.

This would be a perfect ending to a horrible story. I could carry on my own, accept the sympathies of everyone genuinely believing we had lost a loving father and husband. I wouldn't have said a word, never telling anyone about what he had done and who he really was. I would have held my head high and become everything the kids needed me to be. A start to my life after being held down in the shadows for too long.

He was staring at me, waiting for a reaction. Sometimes I believed it was scarier that he expected me to care, that somewhere inside of him he thought that I loved him or cared at all about him. That privilege was lost many years ago, that ability to care at all for him or his wellbeing had been revoked. I actively prayed for his downfall. But he expected me to play along and pretend to be scared at the thought of him killing himself. He obviously didn't get the reaction he had been wanting as he stormed off without saying anything else.

I stood there and knew that I'm not lucky enough for him to go through with killing himself.

Still folding laundry and organising the clothes in the bedrooms upstairs, he came back to me a little later. There was an A4 piece of paper in his hand, lined and obviously torn out of the notepad that he used to work out the money and bills which he obsessively updated multiple times a day. The page was filled with words written in his messy scrawl. I sighed knowing that whatever he had taken the time to write would have been for nothing because I could never read his handwriting.

As he thrust the paper into my hand, dramatically walking away he told me he was leaving, he was taking the car and would never be back. There were more words, but my heart exploded in delight at the possibility that this could be true. Could I be so lucky? I wanted it to be true too badly but knew that he was just playing another game. See how I would react.

Well, part of me felt guilty as he slammed the front door shut and I eventually heard the noise of the car driving away.

If he did kill himself and I had known, then I would be to blame if I didn't raise the alarm for any concerns I had. What did you do in this situation? Phone the police, his parents? I knew that was the right thing to do and something that I would have done for anyone else. I take suicide seriously, I know the dark depths of wanting to die, I felt them often, most days in fact that shadow crossed the back of my eyes, clouding my thoughts and tainting my feelings and memories.

I have sympathy for anyone who has ever felt like that and would never invalidate anyone's experiences BUT I knew with him that he would never risk his life. People like him toy with people's emotions and he was using my own experiences against me here. He was trying to play to my empathy and compassion.

He would come home and no doubt I'd be in trouble later for not acting appropriately. He wanted me to make a mess and give him attention. I wasn't going to give in to him. The only rebellion I could manage now was to actively act against him as much as I could, I would never make it easy for him, ever. Never let him win if I could put up even the smallest piece of resistance and rebellion. I would make everything as difficult as possible for him. If that's all I could do, then that's what I would do.

A few hours later the front door was unlocked, and I heard him come in. Shame, part of me had hoped that he never would and instead I would have a visit from the police telling me they had found a body. I imagined myself like those Hollywood trophy wives whose rich older husbands die in unexplained circumstances. I would be able to pretend to be upset while with the police, pretend that it was so very unfortunate and however would we cope losing the heart of our family. I'd take my sympathies and then go about my days as if I had never met him. I wouldn't have to play the Pretend He Doesn't Exist game that I used to on most days. It was all that would help my mental health function. He would be dead, and I would be free.

Now however, that dream was once again shattered and he came thundering up the stairs, "You really don't love me, do you?" Oh, so that's what this was about. Somewhere inside his delusional mind it was finally sinking in that when I told him all those times that I didn't love him I was saying it because I meant it. His face wore a look which would have suggested he was hurt but really, he was inconvenienced because I didn't play his game. He wanted a fuss, he wanted attention, and I had no intention of giving him either. He didn't exist to me; he was dead to me. My captor, my jailor, my abuser. I looked at him and agreed, simply saying, "No, I don't." He went on now, "you should have called my mum, my gran, the police. You should have told them that I had left to kill myself."

I sighed and did what I knew I shouldn't but couldn't help myself. "Someone who wants to kill themselves doesn't tell people they are going to do it. They do it in private, in secret so that no one can stop them." I looked at him now, making sure he was following my words, "You had no intention of killing yourself, we both know that." I knew it deep down, he was not one to harm himself, he thought too much of himself for that. The thought would never genuinely enter his head, what he had done, he had done as a game, nothing more. He began talking and making a fuss, being argumentative but I drowned out as much of what he was saying as possible.

I had become accustomed over the years to the lies and deceptions, knowing full well that neither of us believed what he was saying. He didn't care though, that was part of what made him so bizarre to me. How could he lie so easily and keep going even when people didn't believe him. I didn't believe him, others believed the confidence he showed in what he had to say. Well, experience with him had taught me better.

Still to this day, his death is something I know would solve most problems that I have.

THE FINAL YEAR!

★ ★ ★ ★ ★

2019!

Alcohol and turning fully sober

Unknown to me then this would be the last time that I would ever be drunk. I had a tumultuous relationship with alcohol but at this stage I could have easily and seriously spiralled myself into alcoholism because I needed escape. I was angry and hurt and falling apart. I think, now, looking back that it was visible to everyone. I thought I was doing such a good job at hiding the abuse and yet, now, I don't think I did. I think that no one reached out to help me because no one really cared.

Since we didn't have a lot of spare cash to go out and do things he would invite friends round most weeks, and I was glad of it because normally that gave me a night off from being hurt.

Getting pissed off at him and drinking in front of the company was a small act against him which caused me nothing but trouble of course. He liked me drunk because he could take advantage of me as I either wouldn't fight him as fiercely as I would sober or I wouldn't remember what he had done. Allan always said that I should be grateful that I didn't remember but it was always worse for me. I overthink so trust me when my mind fails me, black out to protect me from the horrible truth of what has happened, my imagination always steps in to come up with situations and incidents that are possibly worse. I say possibly because sometimes I can't even imagine the evil that is acted out upon me.

This was one of those unlucky nights where I do remember and wish I didn't.

I got drunk and insulted him. Flirted with his friend and basically embarrassed myself according to Allan but my mental health was so far gone at this stage, I didn't give a fuck.

I think he was starting to realise that.

He took everyone home; he was the designated driver so that everyone else could drink. When he came back, he found me on the floor in our bedroom, and I was on my hands and knees vomiting on the laminate floor. That's how drunk I was, I was throwing up. I can remember having a panic attack like I usually did when I was sick, needing comfort and not getting any as he stood and watched me. I remember the black dress I had been wearing. I was floating in and out, not quite with it fully but crying and hyperventilating as I was physically sick repeatedly.

While vomiting, and panicking about it, crying and making sobbing sounds, he felt this would be a great time to while I was still on my hands and knees, rape me from behind.

I cried more, I was spinning in and out of consciousness, still throwing up and of course, was covered in said vomit. It was down my face, along with all the snot and tears. It was over my dress, and I was leaning on it. Somehow, this was sexual to him, and he raped me, raped me until he ejaculated inside of me and then simply got up and went to bed.

He left me there, in my vomit and crying, wondering what the fuck had happened.

This is the last time that I have been drunk. Since then, I have had the odd drink, like a cocktail at a restaurant. Maybe two times this has happened. I've had the odd bottle of Kopparberg genuinely trying to just "enjoy having a drink". However, and this is important, I am fed up with being taken advantage of while vulnerable. I don't like taking any kind of medication since what happened with the anti-psychotics. Later when I was struggling to sleep, I would desperately need something medicinal to help with that. Yet I wouldn't take anything because even when I was living alone, I feared being unable to protect myself if he turned up at my house.

Date night

Date night with someone who hates me, just what I need. He had lied to his parents again about them agreeing to take the kids overnight. It was a usual tactic where his awful personality made him get whatever he wanted. Before I had finished work, he had called Natalie and Derek, telling them that he was just getting the kids ready to bring them round for the night, that they would be leaving in a few minutes.

As usual, his parents would be frustrated and confused, not remembering ever agreeing to this. Allan's confidence won in the end because he would tell them both that they had forgotten that they had agreed ages ago, and he would just keep going until he wore them down. There had been occasions where his father had said no, putting his foot down that they had plans themselves and Allan would just turn up at their house and drop the kids off anyway.

Natalie and Derek wouldn't turn the kids away at that point, I mean, what would anyone do in that situation? It was disgusting behaviour and made me embarrassed every time, so I was glad that I hadn't been there to witness it. Instead, Allan had picked me up from work and taken me straight out for food.

The conversation was mostly pleasant as I even remarked how nice he was being. How he was able to rip my stomach from my body with a single sentence was a talent, one that I didn't like at all. He told me then why,

"I don't like having kids. I wish it was just you and me." Right then I stopped eating, suddenly sick to my stomach and stared at him. Not caring if I was making a scene, I shouted at him, "What?" I looked at him, staring intently as I couldn't believe what I was hearing. "You fucking monster, what did you say?"

He sighed, knowing he had upset me but answered anyway, "I don't like having kids. They get in the way, I don't have any freedom, I just want it to be you and me, on our own without any kids. We'd be happy that way."

I couldn't do this anymore, I was fed up of saying that to myself and to him but honestly, I couldn't. Those kids deserved so much better than him and even me in those previous years. They were good kids, happy, intelligent, smart, funny and fucking amazing and this absolute fucking bastard had the fucking cheek… I was angry, disgusted and generally felt so many negative things towards him that I was shocked it was a new low even for him. What the actual fuck?!

"I'm done. I can't." I stuttered for a few moments as I was so angry that I couldn't get the words to form. I couldn't speak. "How dare you." He sat with his head bowed, not because he felt bad, I knew he didn't but because I was making a scene and he was keeping his cool. We were in public after all. If I acted like a psycho in front of others, it just helped his representation of me being insane. That I was the unreliable one. That I couldn't be trusted or believed if I ever dared to tell anyone about what went on at home behind closed doors. He couldn't risk the exposure, that his precious reputation not be tainted by his own actions.

I shouldn't have done that...

He had chased me to the bedroom, blocking and cornering me so I had nowhere else to escape to. I was trapped and unhappy, knowing exactly what he wanted to do to me. Grabbing the baseball bat that was resting up against the built-in wardrobe, I jumped onto the bed, it took up most of the space in the room. I swung it towards him, and he snarled at me, "Don't you dare… Put that down!" I didn't. Picking up the bat had been a mistake, one I'd pay for later, I had dared to raise a weapon at him.

I also knew it was a mistake because the likelihood of me getting a decent hit in was slim, then I'd have to swing again, which would give him room to move towards me. He wasn't stupid and he was weighing up the options, the look in his eye deadly, happy to have any excuse to attack me.

Fuck.

He got the bat off me easily.

***

He had me pinned to the bed feeling vulnerable in a position that I was genuinely struggling to get out of. Bastard! He knew exactly what he had done here and no amount of me thrashing my lower body around was going to be able to dismount him. He was straddling my chest, his weight crushing down on me from above. His thighs had my shoulders and upper arms pinned and he was looking down at me with delight. He knew. He fucking knew he had me.

The anger was roaring through me, and I screamed at him before he punched me in the face. Why he thought that punching me in the face, a move that I had repeatedly told him hurt me into automatically screaming more was what he did to make me be quiet. I cried out and as usual he became angry at me, his facial features screwed up and inhuman-like as he became in these moments. Truly showing the monster within. Snarling he told me to be quiet, and started to unzip his jeans, inching down his clothing to expose his cock to me. Being so close to my face I couldn't get away from the smell.

It was enough to make me vomit, the stench making me gag and choke, wanting to be sick and desperately needing to get away from him. He was pushing his dirty, rancid cock closer to my face and I knew that I was showing my disgust all over my expression. I moved as much as I could, trying to get away from him, needing to get away from his body and that smell. Him trying to get me to suck his cock for him would be the equivalent of me eating shit and couldn't work out why I didn't want to do this consensually.

He was trying to keep his voice low, telling me to open my mouth or he would flip me over and fuck me in the ass and as much as I feared that more, I couldn't bring myself to open my mouth. I couldn't lie there and let that happen to me. I firmly closed my mouth, keeping my teeth and lips together as close as I possibly could. Sometimes I underestimate how clever he could be as he proved to me again that he does listen to me, just wilfully ignoring my feelings and emotions.

He punched me square in the mouth, the effect was instant as I screamed, my mouth opening due to the pain and shock. The scream needed to come out despite my best efforts to keep my mouth closed. He took the chance and shoved his cock inside my mouth before on instinct and against my common sense I bit down hard and refused to let go.

Now it was his turn to be confused and screamed. He screamed loudly in pain, still straddling me, keeping me pinned to the bed. I wanted to rip his cock off in that moment, serves him fucking right for what he had done to me. It couldn't have lasted more than a few seconds before he punched me again, this time catching just above my mouth and nose.

Again, same as before I opened my mouth to scream giving him a chance to retrieve his sore penis.

He jumped off me at that point and I was honestly shocked he could move so fast. He called me a few names, gently grabbing his penis and examining it. What shocked me more was the look of hurt and betrayal that was on his face as he looked back at me before pulling up his jeans and walking out of the room.

No doubt I would be in trouble for this later but for now it seemed like I had a break from him.

Chilling confessions

He held me tightly, not letting me go, pinning my arms and controlling my whole body. I couldn't get away and I was tired of physically fighting. I was slowly giving up, my body frozen as I let him keep me there. He was laughing, and it was pissing me off.

"You know, when you leave me, you'll just end up with someone worse than me…" I cut him off there, correcting him before he gave me anymore of his delusional shit, "There is no one worse than you. There are plenty as bad but there is no one worse than you." He smiled, laughing a little more before continuing,

"Maybe that's true. But you'll end up with someone like me, someone who will hurt you like I hurt you and you'll wish you were back with me."

How could one person be so fucking deranged? I couldn't believe what I was hearing. He just made up everything and lived in his own little world, didn't he? Before I could say anything, he continued, laughing a little more as he did.

"Or you'll end up hurting some poor bastard who actually is a good guy because you will be too damaged by what I've done to you."

To be both delusional and self-aware at the same time was scary. I stayed still, scared to move now because I had no idea what was happening. Rarely was he ever so lucid that he was truly honest about our situation. I had long since realised he was gaslighting me and manipulating me with every breath. I believed that he was only trying to lie to himself now, knowing full well I didn't believe the lies anymore.

He was still playing some long chess game that had a purpose I wasn't aware of leading to some nail-biting finale that I couldn't see coming. I stayed still and just listened, agreeing with him for once. I knew that was mostly my fate, for once I knew better than to correct him about this. I would never, no matter the circumstances, want to go back to him.

In a rare moment he continued, telling me a little more about himself. This was truly frightening now. "I don't feel anything, I don't have any empathy for anyone. Not you, not the kids..."

Oh fuck...

I knew that I had even said that to him before, but this was terrifying, to hear him say those words out loud. Was he planning on killing me? Did he truly believe that I was trapped here with him forever therefore he was able to tell me something so private? Surely, he wouldn't let me live knowing something like that? There are times where I wished he would tell me the truth but this I was finding out, was not one of them.

"I like fighting so much because it's the only time I actually feel anything…"

There was an alarm screaming inside my brain that was warning me how much danger I was in. I could feel the anxiety manifest on my skin, I was trembling, and a cold sweat was collecting. I was scared, genuinely scared that my husband was planning on murdering me.

But he didn't, not at that moment anyway. Maybe he had planned it for another time because he kissed me gently on the top of the head, a soft gesture, and released me, placing me back down on the bed and he got up. He simply left the room and not another word was spoken. He never brought it up again.

Fuck… What was I going to do now?

***

It was only a matter of time until he did push me over the edge. He knew it. It's probably the only reason why he had been trying at the time to be nicer to me. He didn't want the bomb to go off.

Repeatedly he had told me and everyone else that he was scared that he would wake up during the night to me standing over him with a knife. I had in those moments told him that he would never wake up to me standing over him with a knife, he would wake up to being stabbed. He knew how far he had already pushed me, but I think that he knew I was closer to the edge than I did. This was a different precipice I had been poorly balancing along. He was always more aware of my emotions than I was, always predicting them.

I had reason to fear him; he had shown me exactly what he was capable of. He told me more than once that if I left him, he would hunt me down and kill me. Sometimes, he'd add in that he would kill the kids too. Other times he'd say he'd kill the kids and hurt me badly, leaving me alive to live knowing the kids' deaths would be my fault.

All I was guilty of so far was refusing to give up. Maybe that was the real issue, he saw that no matter what he did to me, I brushed myself off and stood up, got up and got on with the day ahead. Sometimes I was down for a few hours, sometimes a day or so but never any longer. I never stayed down.

He prided himself at length to anyone who would listen to him talk about his heroes; Captain America & Rocky Balboa. Two men who always did what was right, rising no matter the odds stacked against him. That is what he wanted to be, but the truth is that he was unable to deal with any pressure or stress. He folded no matter what was going on. He immediately went into victim mode and took zero responsibility for what were the messes he made himself either intentionally or by his negligence. Or simple things that could have been easily fixed.

He was pathetic. He told me that I was pathetic, weak, stupid… It was all projection, wasn't it? Those things were the shame of what he felt in himself.

I however can rise above anything. I can live with money or without. I can adapt to any change. Money means nothing to me, stability I would love to have but it's not essential. Status, other people's opinions, mean nothing to me. I don't care who has a better car, straighter teeth. I only cared about my own family, the one I had created. He on the other hand struggled to do anything without the approval of others.

He needed the approval and validation of everyone else around him. All I wanted was someone to hold me, protect me, respect me and quieten the noise that was always in my head. The racing thoughts, the trauma, the neglect, the constant voice in my head whispering to me that I should just kill myself. It was always there and the only peace I felt thanks to him was to lean into the warm embrace of that voice, daydream about the possibilities of just not being alive anymore and how wonderful that felt.

I wanted to die. I didn't see any other way out. It was clear to me then that death was the answer to this marriage. Either mine at his hands, his at mine or finally killing myself.

He had done this to me.

This is what he had turned me into.

He'd regularly say, "you'd never survive without me." For years I believed him and yet towards the end I started to say back to him, "by your actions, you've been teaching me how to live without you." I realised then that I had been pushed by his weaponised incompetence into having all the skills I'd need to live on my own. I learned how to DIY, I got over my fear of making phone calls. I was the one who did everything with the kids, all the household chores, cooking and made sure the day to day running of the home worked smoothly.

As it turned out, I didn't need him for anything.

THE LAST DAY

That morning, I awoke wishing I hadn't but grateful that I was alone in my bed. That he had again, fallen asleep on the couch after raping me the night before. I knew I wasn't safe. The terror I felt as I lay there knowing I needed to get up because if he caught me in here, vulnerable in bed, such was his feeling of entitlement that I knew what he would do... I didn't want him to, but I also didn't feel like I would be able to fight him if he did.

Before I had the chance to get up and get organised, knowing that if I were holding cleaning products, he wouldn't touch me. He had a strange aversion to touching cleaning sprays like Dettol, more so bleach. I had missed my opportunity by trying to rest in bed for a few moments, the last few days of being tortured and raped having caught up to me.

I heard him get up from the couch and walk through from the living room to our bedroom which was also downstairs. He came in and I froze, genuinely petrified because after being harmed so badly the last few days I was physically and mentally exhausted. I knew that I couldn't fight him off in my current state. I could barely lift my arms. I was in so much pain.

That scared me more. I know this freeze state was my body and brain trying to protect me. But not being able to fight back made me feel like I was letting him rape me. That some twisted part of him would think that I wanted this. I didn't. I never wanted him to touch me, not like this and not in any other way.

Thankfully, this was the last time he raped me.

I felt like I was letting myself down by not physically doing everything I could to fight him off. This is another reason (and I was right to think this) that I felt I wouldn't be believed. How do you explain in words to someone that he raped me, but I didn't do anything to stop him? How to explain that he had done this so many thousands of times that I knew what would happen if I did try and fight? That I physically was unable to fight him? That it was impossible anyway because even when I did try and fight him back, barely did he ever stop. He almost always overpowered me, one way or another, and raped me anyway.

This man at the time was 330lbs in weight, 5ft11 in height and broad. I was roughly 220lbs at the time, 5ft4 in height. No matter how much I wanted to fight him off, even the times when I was at my peak physically, I never won. No matter what I did, the basic fact is he was too heavy, too tall and too big for me to win a physical altercation. He overpowered me every single time whether I fought back or not. All he had to do was pin me down on my back with his weight, I was vulnerable and at his mercy. There was no hope.

I started crying, he came over to where I lay at the edge of the bed. He lifted the sheets, pulled up my nightie and penetrated me while laying on top of me. His body weight alone, crushing me to the bed was too much for me to move away or fight back.

It hurt physically and mentally because he had only raped me hours earlier. It felt like a never-ending cycle of pain and suffering, one that would never end, no matter what I did.

He knew it was rape, he knew I didn't want him to do this, and he did it anyway.

He knew I was crying because he said, "Shh. It'll be over soon."

Little did either of us know how true those words would be.

***

Sitting in the living room, terrified out of my mind I did the thing that I had been desperate to keep from happening. I absolutely exploded in an ugly mess of tears, sobbing, retching, crying, hyperventilating and I told the police officers everything.

My logical mind was long gone, fear and panic not yet setting in as it would a few days later but right then, I cried my sad little heart out. I cried, sobbed about how much he had hurt me, and it wasn't the first time. I was in shock and not in control of my actions. It was like a floodgate; I couldn't have stopped the truth coming out of my mouth. Something snapping in me and no longer protecting him being my first instinct.

Suddenly, Jennifer appeared marching towards the front door and just let herself in. I watched her as she did it, my eyes focusing on her and struggling to understand why she was even there. The officers noticed my change in demeanour as my attention left them completely, the front door opening and she charged through to the living room where I and the two officers had been sitting, talking. The male officer, with ginger hair, was quick on his feet as he realised what was happening before I did. Jennifer burst into the room and started shouting, ignoring me altogether and speaking to the officers, "She has bipolar… Whatever she is saying is a lie, she's lying!" The officer, bless him, removed her from the room and put her out of the house. I was grateful for that later.

I was shocked by the outburst and by her sudden appearance, not understanding what was happening. It would be a few days later before my heart broke, realising that he had obviously called her when he had fled the scene and she had come to protect him. She knew, she knew what he was and yet, here she was, protecting her grandson. Ignoring me, covered in bruises and uncontrollably upset and she didn't even flinch, never even paid me the slightest bit of attention. The family I thought I had, had never been mine.

I couldn't stop the words from falling from my lips. Repeatedly, everything spilled out and they listened and then informed me that they had to take everything I said seriously. I didn't want anyone to do anything, I genuinely didn't believe anyone would take it seriously, it felt fake, like someone would finally say, "gotcha" and they would leave and send him home to me.

I was only thinking about what would happen when Allan came back home. What he would do to me. There would be no placating the absolute rage he would feel at my betrayal, of telling someone, especially the police, what was really happening.

It took days to settle in that actually; he would NOT be coming home.

He had me convinced that no one would believe me that I didn't expect the police to. I honestly thought they would give me a slap on the wrist for wasting their time. Just a domestic dispute and that would be it. Left to wait for him, wait to see how he would punish me for doing that to him, for telling, for making a scene.

There was nothing he hated more about me than my ability to make a scene.

Summary

Toxic masculinity is everyone's enemy.

It's not an epidemic of violence against women. It's an epidemic of men being violent. No one is safe; women, children, pets and inanimate objects. Everyone suffers when someone is abusive.

I watched my now ex-husband be emotionally and psychologically abusive towards everyone around him; friends, colleagues, family. I saw him being physically aggressive & abusive towards his own family; his brother, mother, father.

Violence and abuse need to be taken seriously.

Victims need to be believed.

Publishing this book will be the most difficult so far but also perhaps the most important thing I'll ever do. I hate that so many people have similar stories, that it's been normalised in families and behind closed doors. I see a lot of people online sharing stories of their abuse and it reminds me of something else Allan did to me that I had forgotten about or repressed so badly due to the awful traumatic nature. Or realise something else he did was abusive when I had believed it was normal.

I am easily triggered by subjects around domestic abuse, I will struggle to verbally talk about this, that's why I write. I will struggle to promote this book. I stand by its importance, no matter how bad a light is shone on me, because the experience is too universal and I have an ability to put what happened to me into words. This is the book I needed when I was going through this. I needed something this graphic and literal to push the message into my brain.

I also see a lot of people online talk about their frustration at friends, family etc for staying with someone who is obviously abusing them. How they ask for advice but never act on it. Please be patient with them, they can't act on it.

The last man who abused me, if you had sat me down and offered me millions of pounds to leave him, I wouldn't have accepted. I was completely unable to let go of him, I had my claws dug in and I refused. The denial is that strong. The stories we tell ourselves, help us survive. The truth is too painful to face sometimes.

Maybe your friend needs to be told 100 times that her husband is an abusive piece of shit, maybe it will be a thousand times. They know, deep down, they will know it's wrong what's being done to them, but you can't act, even when you want to.

My advice?

Leave.

Always, every time, no exceptions.

That is my advice to anyone experiencing abuse. The one thing I have learned is that abusive people do not change.

You cannot change them, no matter what you do.

They are as happy as they can be, abusing you.

Yes, they know exactly what they are doing, they do understand the effect it has on you.

They know and that is why they do it.

No, they are not stupid, they understand.

Everything they do and say is intentional and deliberate.

Yes, they are lying to you.

Yes, everything they are accusing you of, they are doing themselves.

Yes, they know why following other women on social media upsets you, that's one of the reasons they do it, to convince you that you are the insecure one. When it's them, they are deeply insecure and need constant validation.

No, don't feel sorry for them.

They have the option to get help for these issues, but they choose not to.

Do not stay together "for the kids" or any nostalgia.

Don't be worried about "how much time you wasted on them" or anything around losing money or wasting time, it's gone, you can't get it back either way. Might as well start afresh.

Never fear starting over, it's a great way to finally do the things you want without compromise.

Remember, they would not put up with it. If it was the other way around, they would never forgive you. They look down on you for forgiving them.

They will resent you for forgiving them (and for loving them) and use it as an excuse to further harm you.

Remember that any messages you send to someone might be screenshot, and sent to a group chat, posted online or used as evidence in court.

Otherwise, leave, forgive them in silence if you must but leave and prioritise yourself.

Acknowledgments

My only acknowledgements will be for both my children who for their privacy, I had tried to leave out as much as possible that relates to them. I will sacrifice myself but not them in this endeavour. I do not speak about having children online or in my books because they deserve their privacy and the ability to make their own choices. I love you both dearly, everything I do is with the intention of making our lives better, happier and safer. I am eternally grateful to you both and proud of you both immensely.

I do not use AI in my writing or any artwork that I use. Everything from writing, editing, proofreading, my covers, pictures etc are all from my own brain and basic ability to do digital art.

I've had a huge amount of support online from people. People who have given my books a chance, interacted with all my content, left ratings and reviews is amazing and I couldn't be happier with it. I am trying hard to accept positive comments and compliments.

The picture in "About the Author" and on the back of the book is from Dundee in 2006, it was before I found out I was pregnant. I wanted to give that girl the gift of having her face on a book that she later wrote and published. I believe she deserves that.

Domestic Abuse Support

I live in Scotland and the resources I mention here are local to Scotland. I have put up a few posts online and noticed people commenting or sending me DMs and while I always try to respond, I have buckets full of my own trauma and I am not always in a place to respond, especially in a way that you might be expecting.

You probably don't want my advice on how to deal with an abuser; it would most likely lead to jail time… Or an involuntary stay in a mental institute.

Instead, I will point you in the right direction of those who you can help;

Scottish Women's Aid

0800 027 1234

helpline@sdafmh.org.uk

Scottish Women's Rights Centre

Safer Scotland: Domestic Abuse

Police Scotland

You can also attend your local council. I used to work within the Council local office; the customer service centre and we were trained at a basic level for dealing with those needing to flee domestic abuse. I would assume other councils will run similarly around Scotland. They can advise around benefits, applying for housing, get you in touch with local groups and organisations to offer support. They can usually help with homelessness, emergency housing and even emergency cash & food if you find yourself literally out of your home with nothing but the clothes on your back.

About the Author

T. L. MacRae is a fairy warrior princess from Fife, Scotland. Told too often that her head was in the clouds, she lost touch with reality somewhere around tea parties and chasing unicorns. She created realms of her own and lives there instead.

She writes horror, romance, poetry and now non-fiction. Using her writing she wants to raise awareness around domestic abuse and mental health. She believes that writing gives her a voice otherwise silenced by those who benefited from that quiet.

If you would like to connect or receive updates on projects, please follow @tlmacraeauthor on Instagram and TikTok.

https://linktr.ee/tlmacraeauthor

Printed in Dunstable, United Kingdom